Rescue Tails

Taken from the thoughts, diaries, and journals of foster dogs as they wait for their forever homes

as told to

Darcy Nybo

by Missy Sassy Pants and other dogs

Copyright © 2024 by Darcy Nybo

All rights reserved. No part of this publication may be reproduced, stored in a retrieval system, or transmitted in any form or by any means, electronic, mechanical, photocopying, recording, or otherwise, without written permission by the publisher.

For information regarding permission please email Artistic Warrior: publisher@artisticwarrior.com For bulk and wholesale orders please email Artistic Warrior Publishing @ publisher@artisticwarrior.com

ISBN: 978-1-987982-70-1 (Paperback)
       978-1-987982-71-8 (eBook)

Written by Darcy Nybo
Book Design by Artistic Warrior
First Edition

NOTE: While this is a work of fiction, all the dogs in this book are real. There are hundreds of thousands more stories out there, these are only a few of them.

An Artistic Warrior Publication
artisticwarrior.com

Dedication

*This book is for Coco, Maggie, Jackson, and Missy
and all the dogs I've fostered.
Thank you for leaving my heart with
more love than when you found it.
You are missed and never far from my thoughts.*

*Special thanks to all dog lovers, rescue organizations,
and amazing people who foster dogs
so they have a safe space to land
before they find their forever homes.*

~ ~ ~ ~

*"It came to me that every time I lose a dog they
take a piece of my heart with them. And every
new dog who comes into my life gifts me with
a piece of their heart. If I live long enough,
all the components of my heart will be dog,
and I will become as generous and loving as they are."*

~ Unknown

Table of Contents

Author's Note 1
Introduction by Missy 5
Dorie/Dorita 9
Rowdy 13
Rosie Posey 17
Ruby-Roo 35
Bailey 39
Wirly aka Sammy 43
Simon (Lonnie) the Timid Warrior: Part 1 53
Sprite 89
Simon (Lonnie) the Timid Warrior: Part 2 93
Wylie 101
Simon (Lonnie) the Timid Warrior: Part 3 105
Sedona 129

Darcy Nybo

Dogs are our link to paradise. They don't know evil or jealousy or discontent. To sit with a dog on a hillside on a glorious afternoon is to be back in Eden, where doing nothing was not boring—it was peace.

Milan Kundera

Rescue Tails

You can't change a dog's past,

but you can rewrite its future.

Darcy Nybo

Author's Note

I hope you enjoy this little book of stories by foster dogs. I've been the full-time guardian of a few dogs in my lifetime, and all came from somewhere unique. A friend's dog had puppies, a pet store waif, an SPCA rescue, and a rescue association dog. I loved them all as deeply as one can love a dog.

After Missy, my last dog, died, I was beyond grief. My mother died the week before and I was suddenly without any responsibilities. They say grief is the absence of having a place to put your love. I believe that to be true and I had so much love to give and nowhere to put it.

I took a few months to recover and then I made the decision not to get another dog. Instead, I would give other dogs a safe space to decompress, learn to be dogs again, and get them ready for their forever homes.

I know some people think fostering would be too hard, that you'd want to keep every dog, and you'd be right. But when I weighed my options, I realized I could help more than one or two dogs by fostering. You see, Missy, my last love, was a breeder dog for the dog meat industry in Korea. She was socialized by fosters before she came to me. I wanted to pay that forward to someone else.

As for the dogs I've fostered, every one of them has left a little piece of their heart with me, and I hope, by the time I depart this realm, my heart will be a hundred percent dog.

I volunteer/foster through Paws It Forward out of the Okanagan in British Columbia, Canada. They are an amazing group who take in unwanted dogs from all over North America. Some come from high-kill shelters in Los Angeles, some come from Manitoba, and many come from all over British Columbia. It doesn't really matter where they come from, what matters is they are being cared for by fosters so they can be adopted by people who love them.

Some dogs have horrific pasts in breeding and hoarding situations. Some were abused, and some were bait animals. Others had wonderful homes, but due to circumstances, had to find a new forever home.

Please, if you want to get a dog, get a rescue. There's been an epidemic of unwanted dogs since COVID. Add to that the wildfires in California and Canada and you have a dire situation. If you have the time and space and a good heart, they really need you.

This book was so much fun to write with help from the dogs I fostered or learned about. All but Sedona were fostered by me. She was fostered by some other amazing people who let me share her story.

These are their words as told by them. Or they dictated it to me telepathically, or Missy helped me. You believe whatever you like, as long as you enjoy it.

Whether you foster, donate to rescue organizations, or volunteer, it's all deeply appreciated. Even buying this book helps out a dog or two. Partial proceeds of the sale of this book will be given to rescue organizations.

*If you have a dog, you will most likely outlive it;
to get a dog is to open yourself to profound joy and,
prospectively, to equally profound sadness.*

Marjorie Garber

*The greatness of a nation and its moral progress
can be judged by the way its animals are treated.*

Gandhi

Introduction by Missy

Hi there. My name is Missy. My mom used to call me Missy Sassy Pants because of my swagger. (MSP for short) And I guess I was a little bit sassy to begin with, but not after I got to know her. She was incredibly cool. She even tried to learn a bit of my native language so I could understand her.

My story is pretty wild. I was a breeder dog for the meat trade in South Korea, which has now been deemed illegal. A rescue organization found me on the streets. They think I was thrown away after I was too old and no good for breeding anymore. I'd been beaten pretty badly. My knees and legs were all messed up, some teeth were missing and my tail was broken too. I don't want to talk about it, let's just say I didn't have a great life.

Then my foster people in South Korea took me to the vet and I had a few operations, including fixing my legs and making sure I didn't have any more babies. It took a year for me to get used to people and then I was put on a plane and flown to Canada. It was really hot and I passed out on the tarmac from heatstroke when we got to Seattle. They had to pour water on me. Then it was a long car ride to Langley in BC, and then, I finally met her, my forever mom. She drove all the way there to get me. She told me her other dogs, Maggie and Jackson, picked me for her from across the rainbow bridge. When I got here, to the other side, I got to meet them and I thanked them. They chose a great mom for me.

Let me tell you about how this whole foster thing started. I was a pretty sick little dog and my mom spent every penny she could trying to fix me. But years of living in a breeding situation and then another year or so on the street hurt my body too bad. My mom didn't care. She always told me she loved me so much it almost hurt. She loved me so much that I stopped being afraid of other people and even other dogs. She has a granddaughter who was so much fun, mostly because she dropped a lot of food on the floor.

After living with my mom for a couple of years, she decided to foster a dog. You'll read her story in here. Her name was Dorie and while I didn't hate her, I didn't like her much. She told me she was going to steal my mom's love. My mom would never let that happen though.

One day, a couple of weeks after Dorie came to live with us, a lady came to visit. Well, Dorie took one look at her and decided my mom wasn't what she wanted. She wanted this other lady. You hear about love at first sight, well, this was it! I get to watch from over here and I can tell Dorie has the best life. I'm happy for her.

We had one other house guest, but he was rowdy and had to go. His story is in here too.

Then I got sicker and mom decided to spend all her time with just me. The sicker I got the sadder she got and I just couldn't let that happen.

Besides, my grandma was sick too and I saw how much it hurt my mom. I used to lay on my grandma's bed at the hospice and let her pet me. She sent me mind messages about where she was going and told me if I wanted to come, I could. A week after she left this world, I decided it was time to join her. My body was so tired of all I'd been through. I know I was only middle-aged, but I'd been given so much love in the thirty months my mom had me, that I was filled right up. My mom helped me cross the rainbow bridge and once I was there, a whole new world opened up for me.

Like I said, I met Maggie and Jackson over here. I think Coco, her first dog, used to be Maggie, but I could be mistaken. There are lots of animal and people souls over here. Some want to go back, some just like hanging out here, waiting to greet their guardians when they cross over too.

I watch her sometimes, my mom, and even now, a year after I left, she cries. I want to jump through time and space and lick her tears away, but I can't. Then I send my love and I feel her start to smile and I know I've done all I can.

I also kind of hint to the Paws it Forward people who Mom should foster. She likes challenges and boy does she get them! I even helped her write some of these stories. I can dictate what the other pups say.

Anyway, I'm happy just watching my mom help all these other dogs. Oh, and she asked me to share a quote from one of her favourite people, Albert Einstein.

He said, "If a man aspires towards a righteous life, his first act of abstinence is from injury to animals."

I have to go. There's a Chase the Tail competition in a few minutes and I'm really good at it so I'll sign off now.

Licks and Kisses,
Missy Sassy Pants

*Dogs' lives are short, too short, but you know that going in.
You know the pain is coming, you're going to lose a dog,
and there's going to be great anguish,
so you live fully in the moment with her,
never fail to share her joy or delight in her innocence,
because you can't support the illusion
that a dog can be your lifelong companion.
There's such beauty in the hard honesty of that,
in accepting and giving love while always aware
that it comes with an unbearable price.*

Dean Koontz

Dorie/Dorita

Hey everyone, I'm not fancy like some of the other dogs. I don't write journals or type in diaries. I just want to tell you my tale and Missy is helping me.

My first week away from what I thought was my forever home was pretty scary. I was living with a few dozen other dogs, most of them related to me in one way or the other. I can't say I was sad, but I was always hungry. There were a lot of dogs and not a lot of food.

Getting a pet or a tummy rub from my guardian wasn't in the cards either. Other dogs were bigger and pushier so I never really got a good chin scratch or head pat unless I rubbed up against some of my litter mates.

Then one day something strange happened. These people came with all these cages and started putting all my family in them. Mom, dad, sisters, brothers, aunts, uncles, and cousins were all picked up and put into travel kennels and placed in a van. I was pretty scared, but at the same time they fed me really good food and I even got some pets and chin scratches. The place they put us was loud and scary, but it didn't last long.

I was transferred to a kennel in another car. We went for a long drive and finally, we stopped. There was lots of barking and people and it felt like chaos. Then I was put in another car and taken to this lady's house. I met Missy there.

Yes, I will admit I did try to steal her place in her mom's heart, but she wasn't having any of it. She wasn't mean to me, just let me know that her mom was hers, not mine. Missy's mom petted me, fed me, and walked me and told me I was a good girl, but it was Missy who got to sleep with her at night.

She did get frustrated with me though. She'd take me outside and Missy would pee and I would cover it with my pee. Then we'd go inside and I'd pee beside Missy's food dish. I mean, why not, right? Where I came from we peed where we wanted to.

This foster mama was having none of that. She took me outside every two hours and if she caught me peeing on the floor or the carpet, she marched me right outside. When I peed outside she praised me and told me I was a good girl. It didn't take me long to figure out that good girls peed outside.

Don't tell her this, but for the first week, I did it on purpose just so I could go outside! After all, I lived most of my life cooped up in a house with a few dozen other dogs. The yard was like heaven to me.

One day my foster mama told me I was going to have a visitor. Maybe a new mom for me. Well, I had a mom once. She was a dog, like me. And believe you me, I didn't need another one of them. I wanted a human mom, and I didn't want to share her. Not one bit.

Then it happened. A dark-haired lady came in and oh my goodness, as Missy said in her intro, it was love at first sight. This lady person smelled like home. I don't know how else to explain it. The energy that came off her when she saw me was like an invisible hug swooshing across the room.

I ran right up to her and wagged my tail. It was like we knew each other from before. Then we sat down and she talked to me and petted me and I knew. Yes, I knew, right then and there, this was a good thing. This human would be my mom and I would love her to pieces.

And, to tell you the truth. I do. I have a great home now with a nice yard. We go for walks, sometimes with other dogs. I'm okay with the other dogs, as long as I know they won't be staying. After all, I spent several of my best years living in crowded living quarters and I'm not about to give up what I have now.

If I hadn't been taken from my crowded family home, driven for hours to a new place, and stayed with my foster lady and Missy, I never would have found my forever home. And I'm pretty darn glad I did.

Thank you Paws It Forward for getting me a human mom and a safe place to live out my life.

Dorie aka Dorita,
Home at Last

Everybody should have a shelter dog. It's good for the soul.

Paul Shaffer

Rowdy

Let's get something straight right from the get-go. I'm grown up now, and I'm not like I was back then. Missy visited my dreams and asked me to tell you about the time I stayed with the lady and her.

I'm not using my real name. It's an alias to protect my family. I'm a German Shepherd mix, and no, I won't let them put my picture up. Think of it like witness protection and leave it at that. I had a troubled youth but I won't let it define me.

There was this lady who said she'd take me in as a foster dog. I think she forgot what puppies were like. Especially puppies that were the size of her dog. That would be Missy.

I came from Manitoba in the winter, and after a couple of long days in a van, I had a lot of pent-up pup energy, if you know what I mean. When the lady saw me, I could see she was a little wary, but I wagged my tail and licked her face, and off we went to her house.

This is where my need for anonymity comes in. You see I was, what can only be described as, a bit of a jerk. I rampaged through the house and peed on every surface I could find. Yes, I'd peed outside but I saved some up just in case.

Once the lady was finished cleaning up my messes Missy told her I was being a donkey. Well, not that word, but it began with Jack. Remember, I was young, and I'd been in a van for a long time. Before that, I lived outside and we peed wherever we wanted.

I kept nipping at Missy's feet and face and the lady kept telling me to "no," but geez, c'mon, I had lots of energy to get out.

After a couple of non-stop hours of the lady telling me to stop biting her dog and stop peeing, the lady gave up. She sent a text and said I wasn't a good fit.

You know what, she was right. I did not fit in there. I needed funner dogs and funner people. I needed a home that liked my rowdy, puppy energy.

The nice people from Paws It Forward understood and found me another place. In the morning the lady took me there. Oh, the smells! There was another dog there, smaller and even older than Missy.

I tried to play with her too. I won't go into detail, but you can probably guess I blew that too. Not that I was a bad dog, I just had too much energy.

The next day the foster folks found me another place to stay and I did well there. They had younger energy and they loved puppies, and really, I was barely three months old at the time and I needed someone to show me the ropes.

Thanks to my fosters, I have a great life now. I have a family and I love them and they love me.

When I think back to that Manitoba winter and that cold lean-to and my litter mates, I'm not ashamed of where I came from. Those early days gave me grit and bravery, even if I was a bit foolhardy.

Now I have a forever family and they tell me what a good dog I am. And I am.

Anyone can change if they want to and if they're given the chance. Let's face it, no one had ever shown me how to be respectful of my elders, human or canine.

Before I was rescued, no one had taken the time to let me be me, and gently guide me along the way.

It's amazing what a little patience and kindness can do. I'm proof of that. That's my story and I'm sticking to it.

Rowdy (not my real name),
German Shepherd, Canadian-born

You can't help but have a good day when you wake up to the unconditional love of a dog.

Darcy Nybo

Rosie Posey

You would think, with a name like Rosie Posey I'd be some sweet demure thing. I'm not, and don't you ever forget it. I may be little, but I am fierce. Okay, mostly scared, but fierce scared. Missy asked me to tell my story. It's long, but I'll try to keep it short.

I had a home once. It was good, I think. I lived there with my guardian and my sister. We are both chihuahua mixes, me more chihuahua than her I think. She's twice my size and brown. I've got min-pin markings that make me feel fierce.

One day our guardian either left us out and forgot us, or maybe he took us away, I don't remember. All I know is that we spent January in a field somewhere in southern California.

I learned to catch bugs and eat them. I was really hungry. We also had to be very careful and always watch for flying creatures from above. I weighed about eleven pounds when they found me so I was an easy target for owls and hawks.

Some nice people got us out of the field and to a shelter. They found our guardian but they said they didn't want us anymore. My sister was really upset and guarded me like a big sister should. But it made it hard to get food because I couldn't even get to the dish. Then one day some people came in and pointed to lots of cages and started moving us into kennels and put us in a van. I got to go with my sister. It was a long drive but we eventually got to Canada in February and boy it was cold! I'm a California girl. I did not like the cold at all.

My sister made sure I was protected at all times and tried to bite our first foster quite a few times. I heard them calling it littermate syndrome. That's because we didn't bond to our humans and we got aggressive and had separation anxiety if we were apart.

My first foster said I couldn't stay with my sister because she wasn't letting me eat or let anyone near me. She said it was best if we were separated. I cried and begged to stay with her but to no avail. The next thing I knew I was in a car and then all drowsy in a big room and then some lady was going to pet me and another lady said, "I wouldn't do that if I were you."

When I came out of my woozy state I was in some house with another foster lady. I did not like her at first, oh no, I did not. What follows is my way of noting how things changed in my life. I'm not so good at writing, so I hope you're okay with my lists. I just wrote down what I felt at the time.

Week One

I arrived at the strange place with a strangle-suit over my whole body. It hurt to breathe and I thought I was going to die. My down there hurt too but I couldn't lick my tummy. They told me I was spayed.

- Day one: the lady wore an oven mitt to grab my leash and show me where food and water were. I snapped out and ripped it right off. Dastardly woman! I would not eat or drink. I'd show her! I am planning my escape after I release her from her mortal bonds. I hate it here! I would rather die than be nice.
- Day two: I still growled but I let her lead me to food and water. I wouldn't drink but I got soft food and I liked it. When she wasn't looking I tried to bite her foot. I will kill her and escape.
- Day three: I couldn't take it anymore. When she wasn't looking I peed all over her floor. It serves her right to keep me from my sister. I want my sister! And I pooped too. I tried to kill her again, but she was too fast. If I could just get her feet, she would fall and I could rip her throat and get away. Maybe tomorrow.
- Day four: She put a soft doggy bed behind a gate thing in a section of the big room with a TV. She put down pee pads and food and water and just left me there. Whenever she came near I growled and tried to bite her. I will kill her too, and then I will find my sister.
- Day five: It's hard to kill someone when I can't sneak up on them. I'm still behind this gate but I can see her. I warn her whenever she comes near. This strangle-suit hurts. My belly hurts too. A lady came over to help get it off but no way she was coming near. I sure showed her. I growled and nipped and tried to chew on her body parts. She left. I win.
- Day six: This strangle-suit is bad. It smells bad and it feels bad. I want it off but I don't want her to come near me. I think I will kill her in her sleep once I figure out how to move this gate. She does let me out now and then to clean up the pads, but that's it. She tried to take me outside today, but I twisted and turned and tried, in vain, to bite any part of her body. I'd rather stay inside anyway.
- Day seven: This was a horrible, horrible day that kind of ended well. This other lady came over and she had big, unbiteable hands. My foster tried to hold me but I was too slippery.

I felt like a fish on a hook. I screamed, I growled, I twisted and turned and still they came at me. I was David fighting Goliath. These two giants fell upon me like dogs in the desert attacking a rat. I was, and I'm not afraid to admit it, petrified. I may have peed a little too.

This went on for an hour and finally, I realized the regular lady might be better than big hands. I jumped into her lap and a few seconds later the strangle-suit was off and I was wearing just a collar and a halter. It felt fabulous. Big hands grabbed me again and the foster lady took a picture of my privates. What kind of sickos are these people. They looked at the picture and agreed I didn't need a cone or anything. They put me back behind bars and that was that. It felt good to not be strangled, but I realized I missed my chance at killing a human. I will remain more vigilant.

Week Two

- Still behind the see-through wall that moves, but I'm not as mad as I was before. The foster lady brings me food and water. I sleep, a lot. I pee and poop on the pads and she distracts me when she takes out the pads and puts new ones in. I just want to sleep forever. Is this what depression feels like?
- After a few days, I've become curious about this human. All she does is sit in the chair by the enclosure and talk to me. Her garbled words fall onto the floor and I ignore them.
- At the end of the week, she told me I'd had enough rest. It was time to get on with living. She took me outside and boy was it cold. Still, it was new smells so I explored. She kept me on a long leash, probably for her protection. I haven't shown that I want to kill her today, but I feel like I should. Not show her that I could kill her, no. I should just be quick about it and kill her.

Week Three

- She lets me out of the jail cell every morning and I go eat and drink and we go outside. She even let me wander around the living space. When she isn't looking, I pee on her floor, just to show her that I'm the boss.
- She doesn't lock me up as much as she used to. I still go to my bed even though the moveable wall isn't closed. Sometimes I go sniff her but I can tell she's scared of me because she moves her feet. I love to bite toes!
- She's tried to get me up on the couch and I went up once, but she touched me and I screamed at her and jumped down.

Week Four

- It's been a strange week. I miss my sister terribly. The lady says I won't ever see her again. I hate that. I want my sister. It may have been scary in the field, but at least I had her. My foster lady told me that my sister was doing really well and I should try to relax a little. I'll relax when I'm free or when my foster lady is dead, whatever comes first.
- I got up on the couch again and sat at the opposite end. I let this foster lady touch my head, but not my ears, and she can NOT touch my feet, ever. My feet are sore from being in that field for so long. I think I remember mosquitos biting my feet, or something mean while we were out in the dark.

Week Five

- First off, I am still fierce. I am still mean and strong and can protect my own self. However, I like head pats. I've been on the couch a few times and I let her touch my head and my back. Not the ears! She suspects something but I can't tell her what happened, out there, in the field, in the dark.
- The foster lady keeps touching the scars on my face and head and saw the ones on my ears. She tells me how sorry she is I had to go through

whatever happened to me out there. I don't want to talk about it. It hurt. I healed. I am brave.

• We go for walks now that the snow is almost gone. This time she put a halter on me. Oh did I scream! I yelped and cried and shrieked my little lungs out. The foster lady said I sounded more like a squeaky toy than a fierce dog. Now she calls me Squeaker. I don't know if this is a fondness name or a bullying name. I will be watchful and get her if she gets out of hand.

Week Six

• I let the lady touch my legs, but not my feet. I have no idea why she wants to touch them. She said my nails are getting long. All the better to scratch people with. I don't like people. Well, I used to, but not men. Men with glasses are scary. One came over the other day and I yelped and ran away. My foster was upset and afterwards, after the bad man left, she sat with me on the couch and stroked my fur. I can't tell her what happened, because I've blocked it out. I just want my sister, and I want to go home, but I don't know where home is.

• She brought this strange thing home from the store. Like a fishing rod with a string and feather on the end. She said a trainer told her dogs that never learned how to play, could learn with cat toys. Boy oh boy, that's a lot of hooey, well it is for me. I don't like the feather. I need something else.

• The lady had another lady over today. We were in the home office where my bed and pen are now. The other lady moved her feet quick so I dashed out and bit her hard. I don't like feet, any person's feet. Feet kick, feet hurt. I stopped the hurt before it happened.

Week Seven

• The foster lady hooked up my halter again today. Yes, I screamed, she laughed. What a vile human she can be. But, we ended up going to a store that smelled the absolute best, so maybe she's not so vile after all. As soon as she opened the door the smells hit me in full force. Food, treats, smelly stuff, cat stuff, small animal stuff, but mostly, dog stuff. She finally found what she was looking for. Small balls for my small mouth, she said. Well, they smelled funny but it wasn't my money, I didn't care. She also got me a bully stick. She says it's the private parts of a bull. We left and came back to her place and she gave it to me. Look at me! I'm eating a dang bull. I am fierce! Take that, big thing.

- Also, I've decided she can touch my ears, as long as she's gentle. She tried to pat me under my chin and I almost bit her. Not there, human. That's what the big dogs do when they want to kill you. I don't think she wants to kill me, but to be safe, she'd best stay away from my neck. And my toes, don't touch my toes!

- The other lady came again this week. The foster lady told me they were scanning photos because her mom was over the rainbow bridge and she wanted to share photos. I wish I had some photos of my sister. The foster lady told the other lady to wear these leather slippers around me, just in case. She didn't have to be told twice.

Week Eight

- The other lady came again this week. I don't know what this scanning is but it sure takes a long time. I almost nipped her toe again, but the slippers didn't let me. I will try again next time.

- At night the foster lady lets me sit beside her on the couch. I like that. I like having my head and back touched. This week, I even let her touch my tummy. Oh my. It was so nice. Even nicer than having my sister lick my ears. It was hard to explain. It kind of feels like the way rain smells. I liked it.

- At the end of this week, the lady didn't put me behind the sliding wall in her office. She went to bed and left me wandering around. I came into the room and sniffed a bit. Then I peed on the floor. New room, new places to pee. The lady cleaned it up and put me back behind the wall. Maybe that means I shouldn't pee on the soft floor.

• There are these things called pee pads all over the office area. I don't use them as much anymore because I get to go outside now that it's getting warmer.

Week Nine

• Oh, what a fun week this was! The lady showed me how to jump up on the footstool and onto her bed. She read a book and scratched and patted me at the same time. I like this bed thing. It's comfy.

• I learned that the lady puts her fresh clothes on the bed after they come from the warm place. This is a wonderful thing. Sometimes she leaves the room and I get to dig and dig until I'm under the whole pile and she can't find me. She came back in and found me with a pair of her underwear around my neck. She didn't get mad; she just laughed and took them off me. Then she threw more clothes in the air and they landed on me and I dug deeper. Who knew laundry day could be so much fun!

• She now lets me into the bedroom as long as I don't pee. And I didn't pee. Okay, I lied. I peed. But she had a pee pad where I'd peed before so I peed on that.

• At the end of the week, she asked me if I wanted to sleep on the bed. Well, she didn't have to ask twice. No siree lady. I stayed on my side, just far enough away that she could pat my belly. I don't even feel like biting her anymore.

Week Ten

• The other lady was over again and this time I let her feed me a treat. The lady says that's a big deal. Maybe humans aren't so bad after all.

• Nighttime is the best. Once the foster lady is asleep, I sneak up around her shoulders, dig a little and then scoot under the cover beside her. It's so nice and dark and warm. I feel so safe. It's so much better than where I used to live. So much better than the cold field. So much better than a crate behind bars.

• When she woke up and couldn't find me on the bed, she called my name and then I wagged my tail and the bed cover moved. She laughed and said she might get in trouble for letting me do that, but since I was not being scared and not biting, it was okay.

Week Eleven

• The foster lady had a whole bunch of ladies over this week, something called a clothes swap. She locked me in the office. I cried. I wanted to see all these clothes. I wanted to dig in them and bury myself. Finally, she put me in my carry kennel and brought me out to the living room. So many smells! People, food, clothes . . . it was wonderful!

• After twenty minutes she told the ladies not to move their feet and to only put their hand down for me to sniff if I approached them. Well, every single one wanted me to do that so I made the rounds and sniffed each hand. When I went around the second time they gave me treats. The lady said it was mini-quiche filling. I don't care what it's called. It was yummy. Maybe people aren't so bad after all.

• After all the clothes swapping was done the lady took all the clothes into the bedroom and put them on the bed to fold them. I fooled her! I jumped up and dug around and pushed most of them on the floor. She didn't get mad. She laughed again and said she was glad I was showing my silly side. I guess I can be silly. I feel safe here.

Week Twelve

• The lady continues to call me Squeaker. I am Rosie Posey, not

Squeaker. She also calls me Jackrabbit Slim because I jump when I run. Then she called me Puddin' Pie. She says, "Rosie Posey Puddin' Pie, bit the boys and made them cry." I did bite boys, well men. The mean ones with glasses and baseball caps are the worst.

- I went to a meet and greet too. The lady put on my halter, and yes, I screamed. I hate this thing. She touched me and picked me up and I didn't bite. She just kept telling me I was being dramatic. Well heck ya! It feels like a strangle suit and I wouldn't say I like it. Then I get to go for walks when it's on, so that's okay. That day we went to a store that smelled like the store where I got my bully sticks and my balls. There were some dogs there that I liked, and there were so many people. I wanted to bite them all! Feet, everywhere! The lady picked me up and we stayed for an hour but then I had to leave. Too many feet!

Week Thirteen

- Another lady came to visit. She walked slowly. I liked that. She sat on the deck outside and fed me treats. I liked that too. Two other ladies were there, with one of them talking about adoption procedures and stuff. My foster lady asked if there was a yard because I love to run. She told them I could run from the side of the deck to the side yard, around the bush, and back to the tree in seven seconds. Yeah, I'm that fast! I heard the older lady say she didn't have a fenced yard and I felt my foster lady's energy change. I'm not sure why.

- Later this week, my foster lady told me I wasn't going with the nice slow walker. There was no fenced yard so I was staying with her for a bit. She told me I was a special girl and needed a special family who understood my special needs.

- I've got the under-the-covers thing down pat now. Sometimes I don't even wait for her to fall asleep. As soon as tummy rubs are done, I'm under the covers and snoring. I like this place. I'm glad I didn't kill her after all.

- More people were visiting this week too. They had yummy smelling things and I stood by the table hoping they'd drop some. They didn't.
- The lady taught me to sit and stay this week too. I'm pretty good at it, as long as there's a treat at the end of it.
- Something new happened too. My foster lady left me for a few days and a different lady came and lived in my space. She was nice. I've visited her a few times before at her place and I like her. The first night she slept in the spare room without me. But by the second night, I decided I wanted to not be alone so I jumped up and slept at the foot of the bed. The foster lady came home later the next day and I got to sleep with her again.

Week Fourteen

- It's been an adventure, that's for sure. I have a hectic life right now. I still miss my sister but I get to go on car rides and visit other people's houses, and they smell fun. I'm not too sure about other dogs still, but I'm usually up for a good butt sniff.
- The lady says she thinks I'm ready to find a home soon. I think I'm fine where I am. I can do zoomies in the yard, she feeds me, and she lets me sleep under the covers. Why would I leave?
- She talking about another meet-and-greet adoption event and she wants me to be on my best behaviour. Hey, I'll behave in the way I read the room. If there's danger, Ima gonna bite something.

Week Fifteen

- The lady is getting worried about me. I try and tell her not to worry. She says I have to start trusting more or no one will want a nippy dog. Heck, I'll nip those toes if they get close to me. I don't take feet lightly. They kick and I am never going to be kicked again.
- Some hawks circle above my yard. The lady says I'm not allowed

outside alone because in the day there are hawks and coyotes nearby and at night there are owls and coyotes. Like, how is she going to save me? I've roughed it in a field lady, I can take care of myself. Heck, I see them before she does. Still, it's nice to have company in the yard.

- We went for another visit to the nice lady's place. The one who stayed here with me. I like it there. They tell me they love me and I'm beautiful. I don't believe them.

- I think the man likes me because I look like his other dog. I'm not that dog mister, don't try to sweet talk me, okay? Well, at least they have a nice pee and poop area for me, but the lady still keeps me on a leash when I'm in there. Oh, captivity can be unpleasant at times.

Week Sixteen

- The foster lady said she's going to put my picture on the computer so people can see what a sweetheart I am. Well, I can be nice, but mostly to women, and only ones that move slowly and don't get me with their feet. Speaking of feet, I let the foster lady touch my feet now. I mean, the whole nose-to-tail rub down really does need to include feet, but just briefly, and then I pull away.

- The lady laughs more now when we are together. I've been showing her how clever I am. We were sitting outside and the buzzy insects came out and she was slapping her arm and I said, hold on, watch this. I jumped up on the outdoor couch and waited. Sure enough, a buzzy thing came along and I snapped it right up. Yum! She didn't know how talented I was. I had to eat bugs in the field so I got pretty good at finding them and even snapping them out of the air. I am a fierce survivor.

- Other flying things come into the house. I guess that's what happens in this cold country in spring. I decided to make myself useful and hunt a fly. It took me twenty minutes and lots of patience, but oh my dog, I got it. Pretty tasty too. The lady says I'm a great bug hunter. I like that. Rosie Posey, Bughunter. It has a nice ring. Better than Jackrabbit Slim.

• I'm getting used to my foster's routine now. I don't follow her around anymore. I lead. I know when she goes pee, to the kitchen for food, into her office, and when she goes to bed. Sometimes, if she watches TV for too long, I just go to bed and go to sleep. Then, once she's in bed, I slip under the covers and snuggle in for a good night's sleep. I do love undercover snuggles.

Week Seventeen

• The foster lady got excited and said that because it was going to be harder than usual to find me a forever home, they lowered my adoption fee. I'm not sure what that means, but I think it has something to do with them paying all my medical bills and food and such and not getting much back once I get adopted.

• More people came over to meet me, friends of the lady. But I didn't like them, nope, not at all. One was a man with glasses and a hat and wow, I had to hold myself back from biting his big ole kicky feet.

• The lady still puts the halter on me to go for walks and meet people. I still squeak when she puts it on but she ignores my pleas. The human males in this area are all rather strange. They sit in their garages with the doors open and watch the world go by. There are three of them, these men. So far, they are decent. The one that smells like a dog usually visits one of the other two. I get treats at the one place across from us. In the garage beside us, the man there is okay. He gives me pets and I'm okay with that. If he puts on glasses and hat though, I'm outta there.

• I'm letting other people touch me now, not the feet, but ears and head and back are okay. The lady says I need to be socialized and not be so afraid. She says there are people out there who will love me. Why can't I just stay here? We have a routine now, this lady and me. She's nice. She likes to laugh and sometimes she gets cranky, but it's not a mad cranky, more of a tired cranky.

- She took me for a long car ride to another house with another dog and a nice woman and a man. She was nice. The dog was okay. The man ignored me so that was fine. I'm not sure why we were there, but we left after a half hour and came home.

Week Eighteen

- My foster lady is happy this week. She said the nice lady we visited last week would like to adopt me and I get to go on something called a trial in a few days. I'm not sure what that means, but if there are treats, I'm in. She said I was going to go on a two-week trial, on account of my nippy habits and my shyness around other people.

- She also feels sad. She said I've been with her for four and a half months and she's gotten used to having me around. She got all soppy and weird and kept kissing my face and head. I want to go lie down and she picks me up and snuggles me and tells me how much she's going to miss me. She doesn't have to worry because I'm coming back. I will make it happen.

- Another weird thing this week. When it was bedtime she pulled back the covers and let me crawl right in. She didn't make me do it. She stroked my fur a lot this week and gave me lots of treats.

- She weighed me this week and said I'd gained two whole pounds. I guess that's a good thing. I think it's because I'm not just eating bugs anymore.

- On the last day of the week, another lady came over with the lady whose house we went to. They talked a lot and my foster lady hugged me and stroked me and it felt weird. She felt sad and I didn't want her to feel sad. She helped me not want to kill people. I don't want her sad. Please don't be sad foster lady.

- They put me in a travel cage and I left the yard without her. I cried.

I wanted my foster lady. Then she came to the car and said goodbye to me. Her face was all wet and she sounded funny when she talked. She told me I was her best girl, her Squeaker, and that she would never forget me. Then she sniffled and wiped off her face and went back into our yard.

- We got to the other house and they put me in a laundry room and tried to feed me, but I was too sad to come out and eat. Where is my foster lady?

Week Nineteen

- The food here is the same as in my other place, and my kennel is the same but everything else is different and I don't like it, not one bit. I finally came out of the kennel and snooped around the house. I may have peed where I shouldn't have, but a gal must mark her territory. The yard is smaller, but I can make do.

- There's another dog here, he's okay but he gets in my face so I snap at him. Back off!

- The man here, I don't like him either. He moves too quickly. He has kicky feet. No, he never kicked me, but he could. He is kinda nice but I bit his foot hard. Let that be a lesson. Let me know when you're moving around Mr. Big Foot. Okay maybe he did let me know, but still, feet!

- The lady here is nice and she says she loves me already, but I don't know. I had the whole place to myself before, but now I have to share it with another dog and a man creature. I don't like it.

Week Twenty

- I think it's working. I may get to go back to my foster lady's place. I've bitten the man's feet about ten times now and I snarl at the other dog. I don't like him and I don't like the man either. I like the lady. She's very sweet and I can feel her sad when I do mean things to the other dog and the man. But I don't like them. Why do they get in my space? Why can't

I make them stop? Sure, it's their house and they were here first, but still. They remind me of what I've lost, and what mean things were done to me. I guess it isn't their fault, but I can't help myself.

• I remember my foster lady telling me I couldn't be mean to all men, that they weren't all mean like the one who hurt me. I don't believe her. Why should I? She abandoned me too. Humans suck.

Week Twenty-One

• My plan worked. That blond lady that was at the house when they took me away, came back. I was certain she was taking me back to my foster lady. But she didn't. She told me my foster lady couldn't take me back because she was afraid I would think I could be mean to people and dogs and get to come back to her. Well, that was my plan, but how did she know?

• I cried and I cried and I cried. I want to go to the foster lady's home. I don't like this! Where is my foster lady? Where is my sister? I feel so alone and scared. Won't someone save me?

• The blonde lady took me to another home. This one had a man too but he moved slower. It was either that or I was too depressed and tired to care. I don't like this place either. I don't understand why this is happening to me. I try to be a good dog, I do, but I get so scared.

Week Twenty-Two

• I guess the foster lady isn't going to come save me. I'm with a new family now and they are nice. They move slowly around me so they don't scare me. I heard the blonde lady, the one who kidnapped me twice now, tell them I need lots of patience and love and to let me come to them.

• I've finally accepted my fate. I will never see my sister again. I will never see my foster lady again. But you know what, these new people are pretty nice too. Nice like my foster lady. Nice like good food and slow movement and soft words nice. The other people were nice too, but I was too mad to notice. This new home is cozy and warm and I don't feel too afraid here.

• I'm going to give this new place a try. I really do want to be a happy dog, and I have been and I will be again. I hope my foster lady knows I'm okay now. I think I'll visit her in a dream and tell her.

All my love,
Rosie Posey

AUTHOR'S NOTE: Rosie Posey was officially adopted by some lovely people a month or so later. She is much loved, protected and happy in her forever home.

Everything I know, I learned from dogs.

Nora Roberts

Darcy Nybo

Ruby-Roo

Hey there! How are you? Wanna come over and play? Oh, this is going in a book, you can't come to play, but that's okay, we can pretend! My name is Ruby-Roo. It's a silly name and they tell me I'm a silly dog and I love it!

I'm one of those not-scared, full-of-energy, puppy-type, foster dogs. I think it's the older ones that get scared, but not me, nope, not me. I love to play. Do you love to play? I have balls and rope tugs and . . . well I have a lot of toys.

I don't quite remember where I came from, I guess I wasn't paying very close attention to what was happening. I was at this one girls' place for a few weeks and we had such fun! I made her laugh all the time because of what she called my antics. I don't know what that means, but I had fun. But, the girl wanted to go away, so I had to go to this other girl's house. I heard my girl tell her that I was goofy and such fun.

Well, the day came and off I went, metal crate and all, to this new place. The new girl, well she wasn't a girl, she smelled older but I call her a girl, was happy to see me. My girl left and this new older girl showed me around the yard. Then she put my kennel in her office and played with me for a bit.

I don't know why I can't get these humans to play the way I want to play. I take my ball, toss it off the couch, or on the ground or off the bed and then I howl at them to get it for me.

Oh yeah, that's why they call me Ruby-Roo. Because that's what it sounds like when I make my howl. Rubeeeee Rooooooooooo. A Rooooooooooo. That's what I do to see if they'll get the ball for me.

Anyway, I was on the couch with the new old girl and my ball dropped on the floor, okay I pushed it there. I did what I always do. I let out an ahhhh rooooool! And the old girl howled back at me. Oh, what fun! She knew the song of my people. We sat on the couch and howled for a bit and then I remembered the ball. She didn't go get it, so I had to.

The old girl foster says I look like a unicorn because I have this curl sticking straight out from my forehead. Yeesh, look at my feet, I don't have unicorn feet. Some people, hey?

Now, I was only here for three days but the old girl, she was such fun. We played ball and tug and we raced around the yard and we went for walks too. We even went for a car ride to get things from the foster storage place. She's sorta nice. I like her. Oh heck, who am I kidding? I like everybody! People are the best, aren't they?

Well, this new old girl took a few pictures of me and then started playing with the picture taker and then said, "Ah ha!" I sure was interested in what an "ah ha" was.

She showed me a picture and said: "See, you look just like a pequeno podengo and terrier cross dog." You know what? I did! And you know what I did when she showed me that picture? I threw my ball down the stairs and I let out an ah rooooooooo! She laughed and told me to get my ball. So I did.

I am a pretty happy pup, oh did I not tell you that? I thought I did. Yeah, I'm about a year old, but I'm still a pup at heart. Anyway, the only thing that didn't make me happy was this cage thing. It was all wire with comfy stuff on the bottom and it wasn't that bad, but I don't like to sleep alone. The old girl put a blanket over the top of it because I was howling. I went to sleep, but I'd rather sleep with humans. She said I couldn't because I was a temporary foster. Temporary, schlemporary, ah roooooooo!

So, after three days my first girl came back to get me and off I went. Then before I even got properly settled back in I went somewhere else!

I was so excited to see this new place. She, my foster girl, told me I was going on an adoption trial and then a few days later, I was adopted! That means no more moving around and no more temporary or full-time fosters. I have a forever family now and I am so happy that I have to howl for joy!

Ah, Roooooo! I'm Ruby-Roo and this was my happy ending story. Stay fun!

Ruby-Roo
Puppy Extraordinaire

I care not for a man's religion whose dog and cat are not the better for it.

Abraham Lincoln

Bailey

Hey, how's it going? My name's Bailey. I guess you want to know what I am too. Well, I'm a dog, to be more specific, I'm a dachshund cross dog. Like that matters. So what can I tell you about my journey? It's a bit different than some of the other dogs. But here goes.

I'm from British Columbia. I had a great puphood and some pretty good years with my human momma. But she got sick and she went away and I couldn't stay in the house alone. I was pretty sad for the first little while. I missed my momma. I still do, but it doesn't hurt as much as it did.

From what I understand, some nice people heard about me and then a kind lady and a kind man took me to their place. I was sad for a little while but then I realized, they were just trying to help me. Boy did I learn a lot about them. The smells! They must have had twenty or thirty other dogs in the house before me. Not all at once of course. Some smells were fainter than others, some were newer. I think there was a husky, and maybe a cattle dog, and then . . . well there were just so many. Most recent ones were boys though. They smell different from girl dogs.

They were the nicest people ever and they spent lots of time with me and we went on walks three or four times a day. I loved it there. One day they said something about a date night and how late it was going to be and they didn't want to keep me locked up in a kennel for eight hours.

The kind lady told me I was going to a temporary foster's place. She would be my dog sitter.

They took me to this place with a nice yard, a couch and chairs on the deck and lots of great smells. This lady had had other dogs in her house too, at least six, maybe more. They weren't there now though. There were lots of great smells, but I made sure I didn't pee inside. I'm a proper lady dog, I know where to do my business.

We spent most of the day just hanging out. She had a home office so we were in there. Then we went outside and did a walk, had a nice dinner and watched some TV. The dog sitter gave me lots of pats, head scratches and tummy rubs. I liked her, she smelled safe.

Later that night, just when it was getting dark, my foster parents came back to get me. I was so happy to see them. I mean, I liked this temporary dog sitter, but she wasn't my family.

A few days later they took me back there. They were going on holiday and a new family wanted to adopt me but there were too many days in between so I went back to the dog sitter person.

It was nice to be somewhere familiar. She was still nice and we went for more walks and watched TV and I got lots of love.

You may have gathered by now that I'm a pretty laid-back pooch, and you'd be correct. The dog sitter told me I was low maintenance. I think that's a good thing, right?

The three days went by quite fast and then we went to meet some people at a park. The blonde lady who helps out was there. I met this nice couple and their daughter and my dog sitter told me this was going to be a trial adoption. That meant I was going to go stay with them for a few days and see how I fit in.

I am sorry to report, I did not fit in. Sometimes life happens and it so happened that the lady couldn't see very well. I'm the kind of dog that likes to stick close to where food might be, and I accidentally tripped her a few times. I was sorry, I didn't mean to.

Not to worry though, because I was what they call in the biz, a highly sought-after doggy. A few days later I was off to another trial adoption and I passed! I'm with my new forever family now and I'm pretty darn happy. They know when to play, when to rest, and when to eat. Who could ask for anything more?

Now and then I think about my other mamma, my foster, my dog sitter and even the family I didn't fit with. I have good memories of each place and I carried them with me to my forever home.

I want to say thank you to everyone who helped me on my journey to my new forever family. Stay kind everyone.

Bailey,
The laid-back, roll-with-it, doggo

The world would be a nicer place if everyone had the ability to love as unconditionally as a dog.

M.K. Clinton

Wirly aka Sammy

I don't know where to start with my story. It's not something I like to talk about. I had an okay life before, or at least I thought I did. I was a stud. That means, that someone bought me and put me in a cage and brought me out to make babies with lady dogs. Then it was back into the cage until the next time. I mean it felt good, but there was a lot of time in between to just think.

My foster thinks I was a COVID dog. You know what that means? It's when people got cute little dogs like me and bred them to get puppies to sell. There were an awful lot of puppies born from late 2020 to 2023.

Then the people who had the breeding dogs didn't have as many customers, so they surrendered us and even the dogs that I helped make. I met lots of dogs like that. Breeder dogs and dogs that the owners no longer wanted because restrictions were over and they wanted to travel and go do things and dogs got in their way. That's how I ended up in a high-kill shelter. That means I was sentenced to death. And what for? All I did was be born.

I hated the cage where I used to live. In fact, I hate all cages. I used to rip at it with my teeth and unfortunately, a few teeth ripped out of me because I did that. I got fed once a day. I pooped and peed in my cage and when it came time to clean my cage they just sprayed water in it. To this day I hate the hose.

But, that was then, I want to tell you about how I came to the now.

I was so scared at that shelter. One minute my neighbour dogs would be there in their cages, and the next there was howling and barking and then they were gone. I hated it there. It smelled like desperation and death.

They took my picture and sent it somewhere and a few days later these people came from Canada and pointed to the different cages. They took us out of our cages, put us in travel kennels and loaded us up in a van. I thought for sure this was the end. I thought they were taking us to be unalived.

It took a few days with lots of potty breaks and walks in between but we made it up to Canada and Kelowna, BC.

The first time I saw my first foster she almost cried. Someone was holding me, trying to get a collar on me and there were so many matts on my body they hurt. She was my supporter and my defender, and I fell in love right away. I think she did too.

The first night we just sat on the floor in her house and she cut the matts off my body. It took over three hours and when she was done, I felt so much better. She showed me one that she took off my ear that was almost as long as my tail! She filled a plastic bag with it all and said I probably lost weight because of the haircut. We just sat on the floor and she brushed me, cut matts off and brushed me some more. I was tired and so was she so she put me to bed in my kennel. I hated it of course, but she put it in her room so I could see her and that wasn't so bad. I was exhausted and had a good sleep.

The next day was great! She bathed me and dried me off and cut off even more matts. Then she wrapped me up in a big towel like I was a baby and cuddled me until I fell asleep. It felt so good! Never in my life have I felt so safe. I didn't want it to end.

The next night I cried and howled. I could see my defender, but I needed to be near her. I kept remembering the sounds of the other place and the smells and I'd wake up crying. She took pity on me and let me up on the bed. I snuggled right into her and slept the whole night without any accidents!

Now, there were some of what she calls accidents. I don't think I ever lived in a proper house before and I didn't know I wasn't allowed to pee on the soft floor or the hard floor. She'd say, no, and take me outside and then when I peed she'd praise me and call me a good boy. I liked that. I'm a good boy and a smart boy and it didn't take me long to learn that peeing and pooping belong in the outside space.

That first week was fabulous! I got to go on walks and I was quick to learn the leash even if I pulled a little bit. I got to meet the neighbours too. Some had treats, some had comfy chairs to sit in and get pats, and others had dogs I could play with. It was wonderful and I loved every second of it. I was still a bit frightened to be on my own but I tried to deal with it.

My defender had people come and stay at her place and I loved them. They loved giving pats and scratching my chin. There was a girl, a toddler boy, and an older girl, and the defender's sister came too.

My defender put up this thing she called a baby gate to protect me from the "terrible two-year-old." I liked him, he listened and didn't hurt me at all. I liked the young girl too and even the older girl, heck they were all great.

I was going to come out of the office area and get some scratches and a drink, but my defender closed this baby gate thing and told me she would be back shortly. Then she told the older girl and the kids to just leave me in the room, no matter what.

Frosted balls did I ever freak out! I was in a frenzy. I needed to get to my defender, my protector. I didn't want to be away from her! I cried and howled and the older girl, I think she was a mom but she looked like a girl, she ignored me. They went outside and ignored me. I cried and I howled and I barked and they did nothing.

I did whatever I could to break free and find my defender. I chewed and chewed and chewed on the baby gate and I would have made it through the wood, but then she came back. I was so relieved I almost peed myself. I cried and jumped and licked her face. I tried to tell her to never leave me, please, never, ever leave me again!

She picked me up and hugged me and then cleaned up all the wood bits that I ripped off the gate. She covered it with duct tape and told me not to do it again.

The next week was nice. She stayed with me or took me with her and we were a dynamic duo. Did I tell you about my name? Oh, I should do that now, I can be forgetful sometimes. The adoption/rescue people got me and the name Wirly was on my cage. I have no idea why. Once my guardian got me she called me Sammy, short for Samson. She said it meant man of the sun.

Well, I do love the sun. She also told me Samson was very strong and so was I, even though I was ten pounds soaking wet. She laughed and said she hoped cutting my hair didn't weaken me. How prophetic was that! Yeah, I didn't feel so strong. She also said that Sam Heughan (Outlander) was a cutie patootie and I looked like the doggy version of him. Great hair, smouldering eyes, and a real lady's man. That made me happy.

So Sammy it was, and I do mean was, but I'll get to that further on.

A couple of days later she said she had to go get groceries but she didn't want to lock me up. She told me to be good, and I really, really tried. I got nervous when she left and I peed on the floor. I even scratched at the back door, but it was metal so there was no way I was getting through that.

When she got home, she saw my accident and sighed. Then she cleaned it up and cuddled me. She told me I would never be truly alone and I needed to trust again. I don't know if I can do that. I get so scared when she's not around.

A couple of days later she left me again. This time she left her bedroom door open. She told me to sleep on the bed and to cuddle her pillow and she'd be back soon. She wasn't. Well, not my definition of soon.

I heard people outside and I could smell outside too, but the window wasn't big enough to get through. I attacked the metal blinds and tried to crawl through them. I bit and pulled and bit some more but they wouldn't budge. I bent the heck out of them, but I couldn't get out the window.

I went to the other window. It wasn't open but I thought if I could just get the blinds gone, I could get out and find her. I cried and howled and bit and pulled and went back and forth from window to window. I was tired but I couldn't stop. She was out there somewhere and I was so scared to be alone!

Then I saw her coming up the walk. She was back! I ran to the door and greeted her. I was so happy. She let me out and I peed and then we went back in and she put some things away and we sat and cuddled. Things were good until she went into her room.

I heard her say "What the f…!" I hid. I knew she was mad. I peeked into the room and she turned around and looked and me and shook her head. "Oh Sammy, this is not good," she said. I hung my head. I was so sorry, but I needed to be near her. I needed to get away to be where she was. She didn't understand.

She found some tools and took the blinds down. She said there was no way she could use them now, plus she was trying to sell her house and she needed it to look good. Mangled blinds did not look good. Off they went to the trash and I was happy again.

Things were great when she stayed home. We went on car rides, visited lots of people, and went for walks in the neighbourhood to greet the neighbours. I loved it. Then she'd leave again.

The third time she left she said she'd only be an hour. I have no idea what an hour is. I only knew she was gone. I couldn't get through the metal door, but the frame was wood. I chewed at that sucker until my gums hurt. I pulled out chunk after chunk of wood, screaming the whole time. "I'm coming! Don't go without me!"

She came home, took one look at the door, scooped me up and cuddled me. She said I had something called separation anxiety or PTSD and I needed to fix that. She called a lady and the lady told her to start small and give me short periods in the crate.

You can imagine how that went. She said she had to go out for half an hour and put me in the all-metal crate. When she came home I'd shredded the pee pad into a hundred pieces and my paws were almost raw from digging. She just sighed and cleaned it up.

The next day she tried again and I was able to bite off a huge chunk of metal from the door. My guardian defender was not happy. Not unhappy with me, she was worried about me. I could just tell she wasn't happy in general. She loved me. I could tell.

This went on for a few days, blankets over the crate, and comfy bedding, but nothing worked, even for five minutes. Then she switched to a soft shell travel kennel. She gave me a treat and told me she had to go to the dentist and she'd be back in just over an hour. That is a lifetime don't you know!

She put a camera in the office and now and then I'd cry and I'd hear her voice coming through but I couldn't see her. Then everything went quiet, except for the music in the other room. I guess she couldn't talk at the dentist. Just as I was about to go completely whacko crazy with fear and anxiety I heard her voice again. She said she'd be home soon and to hang in there.

I tried, I did try. Honest. But it felt like the walls were closing in on me. It reminded me of the cage I lived in before and I hated that cage. It reminded me of the other cages with the other dogs and the place that smelled like desperation and death.

I grabbed onto those metal bars with all my might and I pulled. I opened my mouth wider and pulled again and finally, I got my top and bottom teeth round the gate to my cell. I pulled hard and boy did it hurt. I screamed and cried but I couldn't get my teeth off the bars. I could taste blood in my mouth and I heard one of my teeth snap. I cried and begged for my defender to come and save me but she wasn't there. Where in Dante's Inferno was she? I was in the fifth circle of hell. I was angry and sad and scared and . . . I just wanted out!

I heard the door open and I screamed as loud as I could with my mouth pried open on the bars. Where was she! Help! Help! I screamed and hollered and she finally came into the room. She dropped all her stuff and came and sat in front of my cell.

She tried to get my teeth free but it was too slippery with blood. And then when she did get my top teeth off and tried to get the bottom, my mouth shut and got caught on the top bar again. She just kept saying "Oh, Sammy, what have you done to yourself, you poor baby." And I couldn't have agreed more. I was in pain and I was unhappy and I felt like a baby that needed cuddles.

She finally pulled my mouth open a bit farther, got my bottom teeth free and quickly pushed my top teeth out of the way. Boy was she shaking! Almost as bad as me. She opened the jail door and I jumped into her lap. I didn't care about the blood, I just wanted to be with her.

She looked carefully at my mouth and took pictures. Why was she taking pictures? Just hold me, make the pain stop! Then she made a phone call and that was the beginning of the end with my defender lady.

A little while later I was at the vet and getting pain pills. I split my tooth in half and it would have to be removed. My guardian cried when she put me back in the car. She said, "I'm so sorry Sammy but I can't do this. I don't have what you need to help you."

We drove away and to this other guardian's house. She was nice and she had two dogs. Did I tell you before that I love my fellow dogs? I might have forgotten.

I was pretty doped up from the pain drugs but I still had my wits about me and wandered around the yard. The big dog was nice, I liked their energy. The little dog was a little bossy, but sometimes I need someone to tell me what to do. My defender talked for a little while with the other dogs' guardian. I knew they were talking about me. The lady person said something about a pen instead of a cage and putting the big dog in with me. My defender agreed.

She got all my stuff from her car, all my food and toys and blankets and my bed and gave them to the lady person. Then my defender picked me up and gave me a big hug and lots of kisses.

I think her face was wet but I didn't know how to make her feel better. She told me to be a good boy and that she'd never forget me. I looked back at her and she was still standing there so I went inside the house with the other dogs to see what was in there. I came back to the door later but my defender was gone. Why did she leave me? Did I do something wrong?

The next few days were quite the adventure. The big dog stayed with me when the lady guardian left the house and it didn't feel so bad with another dog there.

The bossy one even let me sleep beside her, okay, not beside, but near her, on the couch. I liked this new home and the new lady was nice too. Same food too and a yard to pee in. But still, I wondered where my defender went.

About a week later we went to a meet and greet, me and my new guardian. She told me I might meet an adopter there, but I needed someone special. Someone with another dog who maybe worked from home. Oh, it was busy! So many dogs and people and smells and feelings. It was chaotic and felt good all at the same time.

I was getting pats from a nice man when I recognized a smell. I looked up and there she was! My defender was back! I was so happy I almost wagged my bum off. She picked me up and told me what a good boy I was and that she was glad I was doing better.

I tried to tell her I was doing good. I had dog friends and I wasn't half as scared with another dog around. I think she understood. She put me down and someone else patted me and when I looked for her again, she was gone.

You might think this is the end of my story, but you'd be wrong. Not long after the meet and greet I went on a trial adoption. The lady was nice and they had another dog in the house. She even said she'd take me to work sometimes.

Here's the good news. I got adopted! My name is Findlay now and she didn't lie. She does take me to work sometimes and I have a big pen to hang out in and I don't get as scared.

I may not remember much about the before time, but I know I will always remember my defender and my guardian and the people who brought us all together. If it wasn't for them, I might be unalived.

Wirly/Sammy/Findlay,
Happy to not be alone

Dogs have a way of finding the people who need them and filling an emptiness we didn't even know we had.
Thom Jones

Simon (Lonnie) the Timid Warrior: Part 1

Hi. My name is now Simon, (once Lonnie) and my story is a little longer than most. My aunty says I'm prolific, whatever that means.

You may have noticed that some of the doggos in this storybook have more than one name. There's a reason for that. You see when we get to shelters, anywhere in North America, most of the time they don't know our names, because some of our previous guardians just tossed us away or we ran away. Some of us come with names, but very few.

Let me tell you a bit about my name. Well, they named me Lonnie at the shelter. Yes, one of those shelters that get very busy and very crowded and then they just put the older residents to sleep. Yep, dead asleep.

When I got there I was petrified, scared to bits, peeing myself, I will bite you, petrified. So much so that they put a tag on my cage that said, Caution. That was my first name after I was tossed aside. Even my medication for coughs and such said, Caution. Like I'd hurt a fly. Well I could, but I don't. Okay not often. Only if they are bugging me. I'm a pacifist. It was just that I was so scared I would snarl and snap, but I didn't draw blood. At least I tried not to.

Then the shelter gave me the name Lonnie and that's what it said on my picture. My aunty said she wanted me and I made the long drive up and went to stay with her. After a couple of days of calling me every name she could think of from Spike to Flufferbottom to Bob, she called me Simon. She chose that name for Simon Baker. He's an actor who played the main character in The Mentalist. He was a broken man with a tragic past who had a hard time trusting people. She said it fit me well. Plus he was blonde, cute and had curly hair, like me! I think I wrote about it in my Diary.

This is my story, as I dictated it through some kind of weird magic way with the help of Missy and Maggie and Jackson, Aunty's dogs that live over the rainbow bridge. I hope you enjoy it.

* * *

Simon's Diary

Day 1

I have no idea where I am. It's been a horrible past few weeks. There was danger, and I was afraid and hurt and so lonely. Then I ended up in the doggy hospital and got pills and needles and there were so many other dogs crying. I was so scared. I still am.

There was another place with lots of see-through caves and so many of my kind crying and howling and barking and whining. Word got around that many of us would die that day or maybe the next. But we never knew who it would be.

I thought I would go insane. A few days ago, I think it was two, it could have been three, some people came and loaded all the see-through caves into a van and we drove away.

The other captives didn't know where we were going and neither did I. We stopped a few times for food and pee breaks and I was so scared I tried to bite everyone who came near.

"Let me go!" I screamed but they didn't understand. "Don't hurt me!" I cried. Then they took me to a pee place and fed me and put me back in the safety of my cave. I heard one of them call it a kennel. I don't care what it's called, it's the only place I feel safe.

We finally stopped driving and the doors opened and there were so many humans everywhere. People talking, dogs barking, and the smell of food and scared pups was all around me. I watched as one by one all the travel caves were taken out of the van. All but mine. I didn't say a word. I just watched. Perhaps this is where the hurt would continue. This could be the place where I would meet my end. I will be brave, I will fight 'til the end.

A female human came up to my travel cave and said hello. "Hey sweetie, I'm your new foster aunty. I'll get you home soon, I promise."

Home? What does she know of home? I want to cry, I want to bite her, I want out! I can't go home. They don't want me anymore. No more will I service the females and continue my regal line. No more will I enjoy the pleasure of procreation. I am doomed.

Then another human stuck her hands in my travel cave. I screamed at her, "Get away! Leave me alone!" but she didn't listen. Humans can be very persistent.

All around me other dogs were being picked up and taken away. Some were still scared but most were happy barks and cries of joy. What was wrong with them? Didn't they know humans were dangerous? I didn't call out though, I was too busy staying away from the human hands trying to put a rope around my neck. They were probably going to hang me. Vicious, vile creatures these humans. I just want to find a hole and crawl in and sleep.

Then, when I wasn't paying close attention, a noose slipped around my neck. Holy heck that was horrible. She pulled me out of the safety of my travel cave and walked me away from the noise.

Oh, it felt good to walk. And the rope thing felt a little familiar. I walked right beside the female human and the next thing I knew I was in a new travel cave in the back of another car. We drove for about half an hour.

I was hungry but I didn't say anything. I waited and waited and then the female human who called me sweetie picked me up, travel cave and all, and took me into her house.

The smells! My goodness there have been at least six other dogs in here I think, maybe more. I lifted my leg to add to the scents and was immediately told, no! She picked up the other end of my rope and took me outside. It was dark, but I could see with my nose. The smells! All new smells. Other dogs, birds, deer, maybe even a marmot, and humans, a few human smells. There were flowers and trees and grass and bushes and I rushed to each one and peed and peed and peed until I couldn't pee anymore.

I forgot to mention, the stairs. That's what she called them. These things I had to go down and up but I didn't want to. What if I slipped or fell? But the lady person coaxed me with the rope on my neck and I made it up and down that night.

As I write this, I am curled up cozy and warm in my travel cave. She put it in the room she sleeps in. It's all so new, new smells all around but it feels safe. I have survived a journey of thousands of miles, and now I must rest my weary head. Tomorrow I will be wary and see what this human has in store for me. If it's death, I will face it. I am a warrior.

Until then,

Simon (Lonnie) The Timid Warrior

Day 2

What is this fresh hell? I awoke to the cave door being opened and a tug on my noose. I was going to fight it and then this voice asked me if I wanted to go outside.

Heck yeah! I know outside, it's freedom and it's away from humans. We went outside and she coaxed me down those strange things called stairs. Then she let me go. I explored the yard and found where the others pooped and immediately added my scent to the area.

After a few minutes, she called me. "Hey Lonnie, come on boy, come!" For some reason, I started toward her. I didn't want to but something inside said it was okay. But I stopped at least a meter from her. Far enough away that she couldn't reach the rope around my neck.

We sat there, me on the grass, her on the steps. She called me Lonnie and I had no idea what she was talking about. Then she tried Sammy, and Buddy, then Jacques, and even Jack. I have no idea who those dogs are. Then she called for Fido and Henry and Curly and Rocko and Buck and Bentley and so on. I was embarrassed for her. Apparently the Paws it Forward people or the ones at the big shelter, had to give me a name, and they picked Lonnie. That is not my name. The name on my medicine said, Caution, but that's not my name either.

She kept going and I started to feel sorry for her. Finally, she asked if my name was Simon. I did like that name, it felt right, not totally right, but close enough. I accepted Simon with the middle name of Lonnie.

I don't have a last name yet. Not until I'm adopted, or that's what she tells me. But there's no way I'm going to live with anyone. I mean, I'm just here for a short time lady, and then, I'm back on the road, a wanderers' life is what I know. I am a bit timid, but I am a warrior at heart.

My first full day with this human was strange. She only put water in my dish. No food. Instead, she fed me, one kibble at a time until I realized I was standing right next to her! Oh, what a fright I had. I ran so fast, but not too far. She did have food you know.

Once I figured if she had food in her hand, she couldn't grab me, I would pick it out of her fingers. Talk about having to eat slowly. It took hours I tell ya. Hours!

She touched my face once and I screamed at her. "No! Get away foul woman, begone!" But she didn't leave.

Then this fair-haired human who smelled a little familiar came over. It all started out lovely with us sitting on the lawn and then, horror of horrors, they tried to put a collar on me. No way! Nuh-uh! Heckers no! I squirmed and yelped and ran as far as the rope would let me. They gave up after a half hour or so. I think it was because I pooped myself. Not out of fear, well, okay, maybe out of fear. Even warriors get scared. I got poop on the rope and the fair-haired lady got it on her dress. Ha! Served her right.

After the blonde lady with poop on her dress left, the other lady, who I now realize is my captor, sat back on the steps and coaxed me towards her. Well, I wouldn't do it. But, when she went into the house I followed her. She hasn't hurt me, yet. But time will tell.

She fed me by hand again and I ate it and as a reward, she gave me soft food in my dish. Maybe she's not all that bad, or maybe she's the calm before the storm. I shall remain cautious, just in case, as any good warrior would. Tomorrow is another day.

Until then,
Simon (Lonnie) The Timid Warrior

Day 3

Honestly, I don't have much to write today. It was more of the same. Outside in the morning, do my business and then watch her watch me. Outside again five or six times and then bed.

I do have one bit of good news. I have mastered the stairs. Once I got the hang of it, there was no doubt in my mind they were safe and not scary at all. Besides, they lead down to the great smells of the yard and back up to the water dish on the deck and the food inside the house.

Yes, she fed me by hand, again. And then, a delicious treat. She sat close to me on the floor and fed me chicken! It was so good. It reminded me that warriors get feasts now and then.

I messed up though. After all the chicken was gone, I accidentally licked her fingers. I jumped back when I realized what I'd done. Dog-to-human contact was not allowed in my before life and I suspect it is not allowed now.

Do you want to know a secret? She tasted pretty good, you know, underneath the chicken flavour. And something else too, I didn't want to bite her. Very strange. I'll have to sleep on this and try to figure out what is changing in me.

Until then,
Simon (Lonnie) The Timid Warrior

Day 4

Well Diary, it's been a strange few days hasn't it? Today is garbage day, or so she said. She wandered out of the room muttering about it being too early to get up. I got a little excited. I used to love garbage day. That's when all the good food was easy to get at.

I heard her making people noises in the other room and then she came back to my travel cave. She called me Simon again and asked if I wanted out of my crate and go outside.

Crate is new to me, outside is not. She didn't even have to grab the end of the rope, I simply followed her out of this crate as she calls it and we went outside.

The bags of garbage smelled delicious, with a little hint of urine. I suspect that's from the pee she wiped up inside the house last night. Well, there were other smells in the house, I was simply covering them up as a good warrior would. I think she was surprised at how much pee I had in me after a half hour of wandering the yard before bed and peeing on all I could find.

Well Diary, she walked towards the freedom gate and put the garbage in a big black container. Then she looked at me and said, "Simon, stay!"

Fluffing heck captor woman. I want out. I don't want to stay here. I mean you have good food but no, I want out. I stood my ground, the little warrior that I am. I waited for my moment to escape and then she moved the big black container. Holy biscuits it was big and loud! The sound of the wheels on the rocks and then the sidewalk scared the you-can-guess-what out of me. I turned tail and ran. That's the sign of a good warrior you know. Someone who knows when to fight and when to retreat.

A few minutes later she came back through the freedom gate and went back into the house. She got some yummy food out and put it in my dish. Finally no more finger feeding. Then she sat down, scooped it onto her fingers, and hand-fed me again. Jumpin' jackrabbits captor lady, I'm not a baby, I can feed myself.

Okay, I admit, I liked her feeding me. I felt special and well, a little bit safer than yesterday.

After food, we went into this other room with a big crate and I jumped right in it. She just sat there with her back to me for most of the day, talking to herself. She had these things on her head and when she was done talking, she took them off. She's a strange person. I hope my captor isn't unhinged.

It was more of the same for the rest of the day. She'd sit with her back to me, then we'd go outside, then inside, then outside, until it was food time again. I admit I napped through most of it. That night I walked straight into my travel cave, or crate, or whatever it is. It smells like me now. It is safe, and for now, so am I. However, attentiveness is key to my survival. We shall see what tomorrow brings.

Until then,
Simon (Lonnie) The Timid Warrior

Day 5

As day five with my captor dawned, I watched her sleeping. She's not even in a crate, how can she even feel safe? I'm tired of listening to her. I won't get out of my crate, I won't! I won't! Oh, wait, she said potty and food, I guess I can come out but I won't let her touch me. I won't! I won't! I survived the streets of Los Angeles, I survived captivity at a vet, and then again with other fellow prisoners in lots of cages and then a long car ride. I must remember, I am a warrior!

The outside was glorious this morning. I have staked out my territory in the last few days. My scent is on every corner, every tree, every bush in the yard.

So far I've counted sixty-eight rocks around the other plants and I've peed on twenty-five of them. It's a lot of work, but I can do it.

That thing is still around my neck. I've tried to get it off, but it won't budge. It annoys me until my captor picks up the other end and says, "Want to walk with me?" I know the word walk and I walk very well on my rope thing inside the yard. But, some birds flap, and leaves rustle and bugs hop and that keeps me on high alert.

This morning, when we were outside, my captor held out her hand and didn't have food. What does she think I am, stupid? Well, I sniffed it anyway to appease her as she wasn't getting it out of my face. I gave it a little lick, to taste only, and it was okay, but it was not a treat or food.

Then she did the most horrible thing! She touched my face, my actual chin, and the side of my mouth. I was furious! How dare she touch me without permission in this day and age! I screamed and then I went to bite her but then something strange happened. She didn't pull away, in fact, she let me put her finger in my mouth. I was shocked! It tasted pretty good but I was careful not to bite down. I don't want to hurt her, just warn her. I do know not to bite the hand that feeds me even if it scares me. Instead, I gave a big stress yawn and my captor moved her hand. She might not be so bad after all.

She put dry food in my dish today and gave me soft food too, so I'm going to follow her around just in case there's more. But not too close. No more touching today, no! I forbid it.

We went inside that peculiar room again and she sat with her back to me in front of that strange light thing that makes tippy-tappy noises when she moves her hands. She set up a big cave in the strange room, so I am safe, but I will be on alert, just in case.

If I survive captivity, I will write more tomorrow.

Until then,
Simon (Lonnie) The Timid Warrior

Day 6

Today my captor showed me a portal to the outside world. I can't smell it or go through it, but it is like magic in that I can see through and bark at the human who lives next door. I must remain vigilant.

I have also concluded that my captor is a sorcerer, a witch, or at the very least, magic. It's the words that fool me. She says them and then something way back in my mind remembers and I just do it.

I noticed it yesterday when she asked if I wanted to go outside for a walk and I just felt, lighter, like walking was a good thing. She's also been bringing me close and telling me to sit, and I do! This is where the spells come into play I think. This afternoon, without me wanting to, she pulled me a bit closer and said, "Sit." And I did! And to be honest, I liked it. Her voice, that melodic voice, always telling me I'm a good boy, how could I resist? She says it over and over again like a hypnotic chant and before I know it, I'm sitting beside her. Not being pulled, not being coerced, just sitting.

Thankfully I snapped out of it or she could have lured me to my death. An hour later she sat on the bedroom floor and did it again.

"Good boy, what a good boy you are," repeated over and over again like an ancient incantation that soothes my weary soul. I don't know how she did it, or why I complied, but she asked me to sit, and I did it again! There's magic involved, of that I am sure.

I licked her hand because she shoved the darn thing in my face, AGAIN! I was going to pull away but I listened to the words and began to believe I was a good boy. Heck, I am a good boy. Yes, I am.

As visions of a previous life bubbled up to the surface, I got lost in them and when I came out of my trance, her hand was stroking me, under my chin. I was startled and was going to run away, but then, something oh so strange happened. I realized I liked it! What is this gentle touch, these hypnotic words? She truly is an enchantress, but I must be on guard. I pulled away. I remember there were others, who looked like her, who did not think I was a good boy.

Perhaps tomorrow I will let her stroke my chin again. It did feel nice.

Until then,

Simon (Lonnie) The Timid Warrior

Day 7

On my tail and paws, what a day I had! Buckle up, this is a long one! It started out like a normal day, well, as normal as life in captivity with a spellcaster. It was business as usual, my business that is. Outside for a potty break then back in for breakfast. But then it changed. My captor, the pythoness of mercy (or evil, I'm not sure yet), didn't go to the magic light box that goes tippy-tappy when she sits there. She stayed outside with me. It was no fluff off my fur so I happily explored the yard and found another spot to roll in.

That infernal rope around my neck was getting on my nerves and I wished it off of me. Then, two others who smelled like dogs came into my territory. They talked to the spellcaster and I wondered if they too were conjure women. Were they here to grant my wish, to remove this dastardly rope from my neck that I had to drag everywhere? Were they here to take me to another place?

No, they were there to cause me grief and pain and inflict horrors upon my person! My captor went inside and left me with these two harpies from down below. I won't go into complete detail but let me tell you I drew blood on the dark-haired one, the one that smelled like goodness, but acted like she would strangle the life out of me had I let her. The light-haired one, who smelled like patience, held the end of my rope, and believe me at this point I was at the end of my rope, literally!

I fought for an hour and boy did I scream and squirm! So much so a neighbour lady came over and thought I was being eaten by coyotes. Let me tell you, I was so scared, I pooped myself and then fell in it. This was, of course, my brilliant scheme, as I needed a backup plan for when I escaped. With my poopy butt and side, no one would pick me up. Humans are weird that way.

I grew tired of the battle and eventually, I let my guard down for a split second and the dark-haired one slipped a collar over my head and around my neck. Now I had two things strangling me, restraining me, keeping me from running free. Dear Diary, I was so, so tired. They came at me again but I had some fight left in me. I dodged left, and right, stood on my hind legs, twisted and turned, and then, the rope was off my neck and they let me go.

I was stunned! It felt so much better, but when I looked, there was a lighter flat rope trailing behind me. I think it's called a leash. I was not yet free, but it felt better. I ran to the deck for a drink of water and drank a whole bowlful, so parched was my mouth from all the screaming and panting. I lay down but kept a close eye on the brown-haired one. She had bested me. Now it was my duty to stare at her and let her know I accepted her alpha-ness.

And then, they were gone. I thought my day would go back to somewhat normal but I was wrong. Thirty minutes later I was in my portable cave and the car. I slept the sleep of a battle-weary warrior and awoke to new sights and smells. I met two other people who didn't even try to touch me. They must have sensed I had poop on me. Then I went for a walk and met a rather dapper dog with the most magnificent scent. He peed, I peed, we touched noses, I told him of my brush with death. He told me humans were pretty cool, especially his. I didn't believe him so I peed on all his pee spots and left.

This new collar thing and light flat rope are much better than what I had before. My captor sounded all happy and asked me if I could run. Run? I'll show you run, I thought. She started walking fast and then the two of us trotted off down the street. Oh, the wind in my hair, the scent of the lake, and the sun warming me, it was glorious! I realized I knew how to walk, and indeed run, on a leash. There was no pulling, nothing of the sort. What a fine pair we were, my captor and me, making our way back to the cool of the shade post haste.

After that, I just slept and when I awoke I was told it was time for another car ride. I didn't care. I was in my portable cave and so very tired. I woke up when we got back to my captor's home. We were barely there and two more strangers came into the house. I stayed away, you can never be too careful. As they ate I slowly made my way towards the enchantress until I was behind her, where she couldn't see. I don't want her to touch me but I like how being near her feels in my tummy.

Then, poof! We were outside again and just as I was getting comfortable, within a one-meter distance of these new people, the fair-haired one showed up again! The scent of patience was even stronger this time. So much so, that I didn't mind when she picked up the leash. She showed my captor how to properly handle me now that I had my special collar on. I was very happy, no more being pulled in for sit and chin scratches. That'll teach the spellcaster!

One by one the others left and it was just me and the enchanting one. She called me and I came, but not too close, you can't trust enchantresses one bit. She just held out her hands and closed her eyes and the next thing I knew it felt like warm fluffies coursing through my body. I lay down and just stared at her. She opened her eyes and smiled. She told me it was called Reiki and I probably needed it after such a busy day. I wasn't going to disagree. Then we went out into the sunshine and she walked around inspecting her plants. I followed close behind because, well, maybe she had treats or more of the warm fluffies. I believe I smiled at her.

Finally, it was bedtime. She sat on the floor again and I thought, great, another pull and a hand shoved in my face. But she didn't do it. She just sat there and held out her hand. Well, for floofs sake, this was unfounded, this strange behaviour. Then, she used those magic words again, and the spellcaster did her best to bring me near. I tried to shut out her words, but who could resist?

"Come here, sweetie. Who's a good boy? Come on now, it's okay." The words of the spellcaster reminded me that I am a good boy and I am safe. I could not resist. I came close and sniffed her outstretched hand and yes, Diary, I let her stroke my chin and the side of my face. It felt so good, but then I remembered she also brought the harpies here who tried to kill me, even if they did remove the rope and smelled like goodness and patience. I pulled away and glared at her. Not today spellcaster, not today.

I shall remain vigilant as a good warrior must. I believe both my caves are protected from spells and danger so I shall rest easy tonight, knowing the one with delicious words won't bother me until the morning.

Until then,
Simon (Lonnie) The Timid Warrior

Day 8

I awoke to the smell of fresh today. I don't think my vanquisher knew it, but rain was coming. She opened the door to my cave and went to the kitchen. I followed, because, well, food.

She didn't feed me though, instead, we went outside. She inspected some plants and pulled some other plants. I could feel her eyes on me as I checked out the rocks. I got three more the other day and then four this morning, plus the far tree. That should be enough to keep interlopers away.

Today felt different, but I don't know why. She of the magic words didn't talk to me very much. I wonder if she tires of trying to coax me into doing things I have no intention of doing. She fed me, dry and wet food, but nothing by hand. In fact, she ignored me. How dare she! I am a warrior, I should be treated with reverence, should I not!

She made a hot beverage and returned to our sleeping quarters. I still don't understand why she doesn't have her own cave. It's just a sleeping mat off the ground. But back to the sleeping mat she went—mug in hand. I hopped back into my cave and watched her. There she stayed with some rectangular object in front of her face.

At one point she looked over at me and said, "It's going to be a relaxing day Simon, so just rest little guy. You're safe."

Then I smelled it. It was no longer regular fresh in the air, it was rain! I stuck my head out of the cave and sniffed. "It's raining," she said. "I'll take you out again when it stops."

But it didn't stop, well not right away, and I had to pee. Out we went and oh what fun it was. I ran around the yard, stopping every few minutes to shake the water out of my fur and to pee on trees. It was cool and refreshing and even the birds didn't fly away from me as I ran about revelling in the downpour. All good things must come to an end. I had to come inside. Well, not had to, I wanted to.

Then the one with calming words, my pleasant captor did something so strange I thought I was going out of my fluffing mind. She went into the big room and flattened herself on the soft part of the floor, the one that smelled of other dogs.

I was flummoxed. This was a two-legged, why was she on my level? Then I heard it, softly at first and then it grew louder. She lay there whimpering, like my cage-mates from long ago, and not so long ago times. Was she hurt? I had to investigate.

I crept closer, cocking my head from side to side to decipher her noises, but they made no sense. It started out being like a "Help me, I'm scared," and ended with an "I'm so happy to see you," sound. Whatever she was speaking, it wasn't any language I understood. She held out her hand, no food, again. But I sniffed it and I let her touch me, but only for three seconds, and then I was outta there.

I sat, my regular meter away, and stared at her. She was confusing me, and this time, no magic words. What in the stinky bottoms was going on? Then she rolled from her side onto her back and lay there, eyes closed, arms at her side, and said nothing.

What was wrong with my wizard of words, my maker of melodious sounds? Perhaps her spells had backfired. I had to investigate.

I crept closer staying clear of her hands. I went around her head, sniffing from the tips of her hair, up her head and onto her forehead. She didn't move. Was she dead? Oh goodness, who would feed me?

A small noise escaped my lips, "Wake up priestess of poetry, feeder of food, she who sleeps without a cave. Wake up!"

Like a true warrior prince, I gave her forehead a lick to break the spell, and I heard her laugh. I sniffed some more and went around to the side of her face. Her eyes were open and she was smiling. Such a trickster this one!

A few minutes later she got up, smiled at me, and said, "Gotcha Simon. I knew you were a good boy. You're not so tough." And then she walked away, back into the room with the light with tippy-tappy sounds and my big cave.

Well, there was nothing left to do but follow. She's such a strange creature, but I think I like her. I'm tired and will write again tomorrow.

Until then,
Simon (Lonnie) The Timid Warrior

Days 9 and 10

I discovered something called a weekend. This is a time when my captor doesn't sit at the light box and make tippy-tappy noises. She sits outside and watches the world. I quite like this. We wander around the yard now and then, and she pulls up perfectly good plants, and I mark my territory repeatedly. I may have missed a few spots, but it rained the other day and my scent is not as strong on them. I found a new poop spot too. It's very private and it smells like deer. I don't want them in the yard so I hope my poop helps. I hide behind a bush to do my business, after all, one doesn't want to be letting one's guard down.

My captor discovered something in the dirt with big plants. She told me they were zucchini and they were as big as me! I smelled them, but I don't know what they are for. She wouldn't even let me pee on them. She said I needed to stand beside them, for scale, whatever that meant.

I'm not sure what to call my two-legged captor anymore. She's not a temptress or a witch or a spellcaster or any of those things that I thought she was. Well, maybe a spellcaster. She still has pretty words that make me feel good. She tells me I'm a good boy and I'm also handsome and fast and smart! I like that. I believe her too! She also calls herself Aunty. I guess that's what I'll call her instead of a captor. But, maybe not just yet. She keeps trying to touch me and I hate that so I run away.

For the whole weekend, every few hours she would just lie on the soft part of the floor, either in the big room or the sleeping room and wait for me to sniff her. Sniff I did, but I couldn't find anything wrong. I even got brave enough to come around the side and give a small lick on her nose and cheek. Her eyes were open so I knew she wasn't sleeping. Being a warrior is hard sometimes.

This weekend was quite a fun time though. We watched each other pee and eat and now and then I'd sniff her hand, or when she was my height, her face. We ran in the yard too! She would go as far away as possible and shout, "Come, Simon, come!" and boy did I run. I love this new flat rope, it's so much easier to do zoomies.

And I almost forgot. There's another dog in the house. It doesn't come near me and I wag my tail and try to be friendly and it wags its tail, but I can't smell it. My Aunty captor says it's a mirror and she laughed. I don't know what's so funny.

And one other thing, she made this food with turkey and vegetables all mushed up. She's been giving it to me with my kibble and it's so good. I got so excited when I saw the container I did a little dance! My aunty captor laughed. What a joyful sound that was. So I did it again, my little dance. It's yummy food and worth the price of putting on a little show.

Then tonight, the last night of the weekend, she gave me some special treats. I ate them, unsure as to what they were. I bit down on one and it tasted bitter so I spit it out. Yuck! What vile treat is this, tasty on the outside and bitter on the inside? Ugh! Then she fed me a tiny bit of the special treat she made and I gobbled everything down.

Now, I'm feeling funny. I'm very sleepy but not enough to sleep. She said something about a "big day tomorrow," and I have no idea what she meant. All I know is that I don't need to run into my portable cave or even my big cave. I'm happy to lie on the soft floor and watch her. Maybe I'll just close my eyes a little bit. I need to rest up because tomorrow I have a big day.

Until then,
Simon (Lonnie) The Timid Warrior

Day 11

Holy cat turds! I cannot trust this two-legged shrew, this hellcat harpy, this… this… human! Today started fine, like the other days with this ogress captor. Out of the cave, outside to pee and then a bite of food.

Except today, there was no breakfast, just some of those funny-tasting treats. Well, you can't fool me twice, nope, the ones last night made me woozy, so I spit them out. Then she took out that delicious turkey stuff and put it in her hand. I ate it, of course, and gulped it right down. Before I knew it I was sleepy again and in my travel cave and the car.

She brought me to a funny-smelling place but I knew there were dogs there. I looked and couldn't find them. The gorgon of agony let me out of my cave and handed me to another two-legged. So far so good, right? NO!

My so-called Aunty left me with these vile and foul people. They cornered me against a cage and stabbed me. A few minutes later I was so relaxed I felt like I'd just mated with twenty females! About an hour later, my rogue captor returned with a harness and a cone. One of the scoundrels wrapped me in a towel and brought me out to see her. I wanted to leave, I wanted to go with her but I could barely focus my eyes on her. She reached out and gave the top of my head a gentle pat and a scritch. I didn't care, I couldn't pull away. I saw her eyes fill with water and heard her say, "That's the first time I've been able to touch him like that," and then she was gone.

I wish I could tell you what happened next. I remember going into a funny-smelling room and then, nothing. I awoke with this huge barrier around my head and a straitjacket around my body. Boy, did I scream when they tried to take me out of the foul-smelling cave they'd kept me in. And my back end felt funny. Not funny ha ha either, funny weird. Like I was missing something. I tried to look, but this infernal cone thing on my head wouldn't let me.

They let me sleep a bit longer and then brought me out to see that… that… traitor who I live with. I was angry and scared and downright pugnacious, to say the least. I would fight them all! Warriors fear no one!

Then I saw my portable cave and ran into it, but lo, it no longer was a friendly place. This cursed cone about my head and neck banged against the wall of my safe space and I screamed out in rage and, if I must admit it, with fear.

I finally got turned around and heard them talking about socialization and training and puppy Prozac. I just wanted to go to my big cave and sleep.

As soon as we got to the wicked one's yard she let me out of my cave. I ran and wanted to go in but she said I had to try and pee. I tried, I really did, but the cone bashed against the rocks when I sniffed them and I screamed. Then the fiend grabbed my flat rope. She tugged on it gently and holy woofs and howls, that freaked me out. I twisted and turned and screamed again and again but no one came to save me. What is this fresh hell? Why is there a rope around my body? I don't want to be touched! Please, for the love of bones and biscuits, take it off!

But she didn't listen. She stayed outside and watched me wander, bumping into trees and screaming my little lungs out. Finally, the evil enchantress pitied me and called me to come into the house. I ran as fast as I could and fled to my big cave.

I tried and tried but I can't get this thing off my body. She told me it was a harness and it would be easier to socialize me and train me with it on. Easier for her! What about me? Oh, fluff and fur, she is nasty. And this plastic thing around my head and neck, why won't she take it off? If I try to drink, it bumps against the dish and scares me. I don't know how I'll eat. I shall probably die of starvation. Why? What did I do to provoke such torture?

Oh precious reader, whatever shall I do? I will think about it and let you know when I figure it out.

Until then,
Simon (Lonnie) The Timid Warrior

Day 12

Well, things have certainly taken a turn, for the best, I think. Last night I stared at my captor, begging her to take this horrid harness off me. It was like hands gripping me, dragging me to the pits of hell. I hated it, I tell ya, hated it!

She fed me water through a tube and it was okay, and she tried food but it got stuck in my cone. It was horrible. Then something changed. I can't tell you why, but I can tell you what happened next.

She sat down in front of me weaving those soft words into my brain. The woozies were still quite bad, but I understood she thought I was a good boy and everything would be okay. She reached for me while holding me in place with the harness and flat leash. Then, before I knew it, she had the flat rope on my collar. She tugged it lightly to show me it was there. Okay, I understood that, but what about this thing squeezing the life out of me? This thing that makes me feel like someone is grabbing at me!

Screaming at her wasn't working so I sat and stared intently into her eyes, willing her to understand, and by the grace of dog moms everywhere, she did. This accursed cone stopped me from really seeing what she was doing and I heard a click and then she showed me my flat rope, that leash thing. I sniffed it. Interesting but nothing to write about.

Then she gently touched my side. I flinched a bit, but it felt good. I stayed still and a few seconds later that dreaded harness fell off my body. Oh, the relief I felt! No more squeezing me to my death. To heck with training, I don't want that thing!

Then she did something strange. She started singing to me, I don't remember the words. Then I felt her hand on my back. I flinched a bit but then she stroked me and continued with her siren song. It felt like when I was a wee pup and my mamma licked me clean every day. I closed my eyes, but just a little bit.

The next thing I knew she was gently scratching my head and behind my ears. Oh heavenly dog, it was magnificent! I kept staring at her and letting her know it was okay. "Don't stop," I silently begged. This was so new, so wonderful, and yet I was a bit scared.

Later on, we went outside in the dark but the stairs were so scary. The cone kept hitting them and I ran, but not too far, because it was dark. I was too woozy to pee and we went back inside after a bit. I watched her carefully as she put my big cave into her bedroom. She made it all cozy with the towels that were already in there. Then she added my dead thing toy and a fuzzy blanket. She said I could go in without banging the cone on the side. I didn't go in right away. Instead, I lay on the soft stuff and stared at her, wishing she would touch me again, but not too quickly. She understood! She gently reached over and started slowly touching me from shoulder to flank and back up again. I closed my eyes. Visions of my mamma flooded into my brain and I gave a little sigh.

I should, at this point tell you, my back end does hurt a bit. Also, I can see better too. Someone removed my bangs and I can now see her. Being able to see better helps with my anxiety.

Anyway, eventually she stopped petting me and I got into my big cave and slept the night away.

In the morning she took me out again, but I kept bumping my cone against the trees and rocks and I was scared she would take me away again. She walked away and let me do my thing. I think she was worried but I wouldn't pee with her watching.

Eventually, she came back and we went inside, and oh my kibble and bits I was hungry. She gave me something sweet in a syringe and said it would help with the ouch feeling back there. She put some food in a dish but my cone kept bumping it and scaring me. I was hangry!

She took the dish away and gave me a different one, but this cone kept getting in the way. I wanted to cry I was so hungry. She took that one away and came back with a tiny, tiny bowl. Finally, I was able to get my head into the bowl and eat. Holy chicken and giblets it was good!

Honestly, it was chicken, not sure about the giblets. I ate three bowls too! They were tiny you know.

We went back into the room with the light thing and the tippy-tappy noises. She showed me a nice soft blanket and I sat on it. Then she did it again. She just sat with me, talking softly and telling me what I good boy I was, and stroked my sides and my back. Then, dear dog above, she put both her hands inside my cone. It was heaven. She had her thumbs under my chin, three fingers scratching behind my ear and the other finger massaging my temple. I closed my eyes and I swear to you I fell asleep! When I opened my eyes she was smiling at me and telling me what a handsome and good boy I was.

Then I farted. It smelled fine to me, but she made a face. Too bad, I needed to get it out. She went back to her chair and turned her back on me. I didn't like that, so I left the comfy blanket and lay down behind her chair. This way I'll know if she leaves, and it will be easy for her to give me pats and scritches when she turns around.

She says she has to go out later, but that's okay with me. I'll just snooze and wait for her to come back. Maybe she'll give me more chicken later!

It certainly has been a confusing, but good, twenty-four hours. I shall write more tomorrow.

Until then,
Simon (Lonnie) The Timid Warrior

Day 13

The ouch in my back end is feeling a bit better today and I'm feeling rather, dare I say it, happy. Today was a big outside day and I met lots of growling things. First, it was a growly thing that ate pieces off my favourite pee bush. I tried to get near it but my spellcasting Aunty shooed me away. I wish she'd make up her mind. She says she wants me to come near and then she tells me to go away.

The second growly thing was a wind maker! Wow, it was loud. It made leaves and the pieces of bush fly through the air. I stayed away from that one.

Then she brought out this thing that she pushed around the yard and I was oh so curious. Again, she told me to stay back, but I was nosey so I followed closely behind as she walked it around the yard. Wherever it went it left a smell of fresh. When it stopped growling, I sniffed it. It smelled like me! I explored one of the round things with my nose and sure enough, that was my poop. My smells were everywhere! It was exhilarating knowing I had even marked this growly push thing and in turn, it had marked the entire yard.

We went into the house for lunch and I managed to eat from the tiny bowl and not get this blasted cone in the way. I don't mind really, the food is tasty.

After lunch, we went into the big sleeping room, but it wasn't sleeping time. I was confused. She had another growly thing that had a strong smell squirting out of it. She told me it was to get rid of the spots where I peed when I first came. I told her with my eyes that I was simply marking the boundary in our sleeping space. After all, I smelled at least four other different dog pees, but they were mixed with a weird smell. She told me she had cleaned them up three times, but today she was going to do a deep clean.

Well, how boring was that? She sat on the floor pushing this mouth-shaped thing back and forth. I watched the bubbles come into it and then go into the growly thing. It took about an hour, and then she put a different wind maker, one on a stand, into the room and closed the door.

She carried the growly thing into the big space and rubbed the mouth across the bottom of the big round chair. She said the previous boy she looked after marked it.

I already knew that because every time I went near it, she said, "No!" in a firm voice. I guess I'll never get a chance to leave my mark on that one. (Spoiler alert – I got it later) I've secured the perimeter nicely and no one will dare enter my warrior space, I hope.

Dinner time was delicious and I had a nap afterward and then we sat outside listening to crickets until it got dark.

Oh, you think I'm done with my tale for the day. Oh no, I am not. I am saving the best for last. It's just that the growly things were quite interesting, while the next thing was rather enjoyable.

Last night, before bed, she sat with me and gave me scritches all around my ears, head and neck. She even did my underbelly, but didn't go near the ouch place.

This morning, after I ran outside and peed she brought me back for breakfast and then more scritches. Every few hours, between wandering around with the growly things, she'd call me to her. I'd sniff her hand. Once it smelled so bad of detergent or cleaner that I backed away, but most times it smelled good. Well, it turns out that if I come when I'm called, I get pats and pets, scratches and scritches and heavenly temple massages.

Don't get me wrong, I am a warrior and I am still wary of the spellcaster, but she never hurts me when I come close. She sings to me, some silly song about sunshine and the like.

Then, tonight, as I was growing weary from the day's excitement, she sat on the soft floor in the sleeping room and called me. I came, but not too close. I sniffed and she scratched under my chin, then my back and sides. It felt so good that I got closer. Then she put her hands under my front legs and lifted my front half onto her legs. Wow, we were so close, and you know what Diary, I liked it! I now believe I am a good boy because she tells me it every time she strokes my fur. Plus, I'm handsome. I'm not sure what that means, but it must be good.

I didn't want to get any closer, as this was close enough and then she gently lifted my back legs and put me on her lap so I was staring up at her.

The spellcaster used her words and songs and I stared deeply into her eyes and finally, my whole body relaxed. Wow! Is this what being socialized is about? I would have done it sooner had I known.

Then she said it was bedtime. But I didn't want to stop the sweet caress of the spellcaster's hand. She stopped and I reluctantly got off her lap. She walked towards the opening of my cave and pointed and said, "Bed." No kidding lady, that's my bed. But I think she meant something else.

I came over and looked at the opening and looked at her. "Bedtime," she said. I wasn't sure what she wanted me to do. She put her feet up onto her sleeping mat and pointed to the cave opening again. "Go to bed Simon," she said. I may have rolled my eyes a little bit. Why didn't she say that sooner? I went in, turned around and got comfy.

I'm pretty sleepy after such a long day. I wonder if tomorrow will bring more gentle touches.

Until then,
Simon (Lonnie) The Timid Warrior

Day 14

Oh, what a day. It's a never-ending new experience here with the spellcaster. Today there are more growling machines. Okay, just one, but it has so many smells. I followed it everywhere. Over the soft places (she calls them carpets) and the hard places. It smelled like, well, everything I've smelled here but in one place.

Then she got out some weird thing and it squirted wet on the floors. I am very attached to the spellcaster now so I followed her everywhere. She told me to stop stepping in the wet spots but I don't mind, my paws will dry. In the end, I believe I made a rather nice map of where I've been in the house, at least on the hard floor parts.

Well after the house smelled all fresh some strangers came. Boy did I ever growl and bark. I must protect the Aunty spellcaster from harm, after all, I am a warrior.

Then something strange happened, she called me, and I came, and then, poof! She picked me up and put me on the outside tall sitting spot beside her. I didn't even scream! I surprised myself on that one. She's never picked me up before.

We just sat there and waited. She said someone was looking at the house in case they wanted to buy it. I don't want them to have my territory. But she talked to me and gave me good scratches and pets and I felt better. I stayed right beside her, just in case.

The people left. They didn't want to take my territory and I was happy.

Later in the afternoon, she asked me if I wanted to go for a walk. Well, I'm pretty brave now but going outside my territory is scary. We went anyway and I jumped a few times before we even left the driveway. I got the hang of walking beside her and just as we were across the street from her neighbour a big voice called out, "Cone Head!"

My spellcaster was calm and called back and asked him not to holler because I was, ticklish, no that wasn't it. I was skittish and afraid of people. He didn't listen and kept hollering at me and calling me a cone head. I could feel the spellcaster's energy get cranky and I got scared. The man kept saying things that I didn't understand and my spellcaster kept asking him to stop. Her voice was soft but boy her energy was mad.

Before we even got to the smelly spot where other dogs go, she hollered at the man and said, "Thank you for being so cooperative." I think that's called sarcasm. By then I was almost crying. The world is such a scary place and the man was even scarier so we went back to my territory. I heard her mumble something about him being old enough to know better and being a man-child. I didn't care, I just wanted my territory. I was so happy to hear the gate close.

Dinner time was great too. I got lots of crunchy and soft food and then she picked me up again and put me on the high soft spot, she called it a couch.

We just sat there, my Aunty spellcaster and me. She did all kinds of pets and rubs and I loved it. And then she sang me a song by someone called the Travelling Wilburys. She said it suited me. I liked the part that said I was the best thing she'd ever found. Then she sang about being tired of being lonely and having love to give and my eyes watered a bit. I think I like that song. I am tired of being lonely and I do have love to give.

When it got dark, we went out again and I found a new favourite pee spot in the back of the yard and did my business. Once inside I was going to go to my cave, but she said it was too early. Then she picked me up again and put me on her tall sleeping mat. She said she wanted to read and patted the space beside her.

I don't know what came over me. I rested my head, cone and all, on her leg and stretched out. Before I knew what I was doing I flopped over, opened my legs, and invited her to rub my tummy and ouch spots. Let me tell you, that felt good. It's not very sore down there anymore, and the rubs and pats felt great.

Then, as with all good things (so I am told) it had to end. She put me on the soft floor and told me to go to bed, so I did.

I'm starting to like this spellcaster. I think I was wrong and she's not a harpy, hellcat, witch sorcerer, or any of those names. But she is a good spellcaster.

I wonder what tomorrow will bring.

Until then,
Simon (Lonnie) The Timid Warrior

Days 15 and 16

I don't want to write too much today. It's rainy and I'm sleepy. I've had two pretty good days. Yesterday my Aunty took me for a walk to the big red pee pole across the street. Lots of dogs pee on it, and there was a lot of information, but it was too much for me to deal with so I didn't pee.

Then she asked if I wanted to meet someone. What the heck? The spellcaster has the leash to lead me around, how could I say no? Oh, and speaking of leashes, I've figured out that I should walk beside my Aunty, not behind her, and I remembered that yesterday.

We went up a steep hard hill and met this nice person. He smelled like dog treats and hugs. We went into this big open room that smelled like cars and trucks and my spellcaster sat on the couch.

Then a man sat on the couch and my Aunty picked me up (yep, I'm okay with that now) and put me between her and the man. I let him touch my paw and it didn't hurt. Then he touched my back and that didn't hurt. Then my Aunty got up and let the nice man stroke my fur. She said she wanted to get a picture so the Paws It Forward people could see what a good boy I was.

Did you know that I'm a good boy? I do now. I mean, I kinda have to believe it because the spellcaster tells me a few dozen times a day. I like hearing it every single time.

Once we were home I got more scritches and songs and nice words. I ran around the yard too. My Aunty laughed and told me I looked like a bunny or even someone called Tigger because I was hopping around. I felt really good. I don't pee on the rocks now because this cone thing bumps them, but I've found a soft tree for doing my business.

At bedtime, Aunty picked me up again and gave me lots of pats on the bed while she read. I like this ritual. Then, just when I was fast asleep she woke me up and told me to go to bed.

What the hecken' injustice was she doing to me? I went in, but I did not like it. No, no I did not. I was safe there before, and I guess I'm safe there now, but I want to be on the big sleeping mat with her. She said no, locked the door, turned out the lights, and left me all alone. Okay, I wasn't alone, she was a whole leash length away and I could see her, but I wanted more pats and pets!

Well, I will tell you what I did next should have worked. I cried and whimpered, telling her I wanted to be with her but she ignored me. Then I tried whimpering every ten minutes or so, just when she'd fall asleep. She'd say "Stop that Simon, it's bedtime. Go to sleep." I'd be quiet for a little bit and then cry again. About midnight I did it again, for the tenth or so time, thinking, yes, this one will work. It didn't. She said, "Please, Simon. I need my sleep. So do you, now go to sleep." So I did. She did say, please.

In the morning, it wasn't as light as usual when she opened the magic portal coverings. She said it was going to be a rainy day. I don't mind, my fur just needs a good shake to get rid of the wet.

We went outside and I ran around again, making her laugh with my bounces. I found my favourite soft tree and peed for a whole twenty seconds. Well, that's what she said. All I know is it felt good.

We went back inside and she said we were going to go back to the sleeping room and read some more. She fed me my breakfast and made some tea and off we went, back to the sleeping room.

Before she could even ask, I jumped up.

She had such a big smile, I knew I did good. But she said, "Simon, no jumping on the bed, not yet. Two more days until your stitches heal." And then she stroked my fur.

For reasons I do not understand I rolled over, let my legs around my ouch spot fall open and begged her with my eyes to rub my belly. She did. Oh, my dental sticks and meat treats! This was heaven. This was not like anything I'd imagined before. This wasn't a little pet on the inside of my thigh like she'd done before. Oh no, Diary. This was a full neck to chest to tippy toe, full body stroke down one side, then the other. She missed my boy bits of course.

We just laid on this thing she calls a bed and she told me tonight I was going to have a friend sleep over. She said more doggos were coming in from where I came from and that my soon-to-be friend needed a place to stay until his foster parents could take him.

I'm not sure what this means. I do like other dogs though. I hope he doesn't laugh at my cone. Gotta go. I'll write more tomorrow.

Until then,
Simon (Lonnie) The Timid Warrior

Days 17 and 18

Life sure is strange isn't it? One minute you're scared and depressed and the next, poof! Life is good. I know I haven't written in a while but let me tell you about my weekend and Monday. Boy, it's a doozy!

So Saturday night, Aunty said I was going to have a friend over for a sleepover. I didn't want to be left alone but she told me it would only be an hour and a half and she'd be back. Well, she fibbed. It took her three whole hours and it was dark and I was so scared!

When she got home she had this other scared boy dog with her and he smelled so good! He was as black as I am white. His fur was as straight as mine is curly, and he still had all his boy bits. Aunty said he smelled so good because they groomed him at the shelter in Los Angeles. I remember that smell because they cut my hair too, and I smelled that good once. But no one wanted to adopt me then, so I came to be here.

Me and the dark dog sniffed each other in the yard and then the spellcaster fed us both. It was really past my bedtime by the time we got settled in. Aunty put me in my cave, which I did not like. The other wee dog didn't like it either. So she put our cave openings close so we could see each other and we slept real good.

The next morning Aunty hustled the dark one, she called him Sprite and Pipsqueak, out into the yard and boy did we pee. I peed, he peed, I peed, well you get the idea. Then we went back inside and he peed on my Aunty's bed covering and the floor. I thought she was going to get mad but she just said, "No, don't do that" and he ignored her and finished peeing. She pulled the cover off the bed and put it in the big machine that cleans things. She went back into the sleeping room and I showed her that while she was gone, the dark haired fella had peed on the entrance to the room. He was sorry, and Aunty cleaned it up and decided it would be best if we all went outside.

What fun! We ran and ran and even barked at noises.

Then we did a big snuggle on the outside couch. Aunty left us there while she went inside and got a bed, food and lots of stuff and put it on an outside table. Then a nice lady came and took the dark pup into her arms and hugged him. Wow, you could almost see the love sparking! I looked at my spellcaster and wondered if I'd ever feel that for her. I mean I trust her a bit more, and I like her, but I'm still a little weirded out by everything.

Aunty explained that he was going to live with the lady and then they were gone. I had my aunty all to myself so I snuggled up and fell asleep.

I swear it was only a tail wag later she woke me up. She said we had to go look for another dog that got scared and ran away. She picked me up, went inside and put me on her bed. Then she took the cone off my head. Oh, that felt so good!

I was about to lick my paws but she stopped me and said, "I really need you to be brave and put the harness on again."

Then she put it on me and I didn't even scream. She made some adjustments and it didn't hurt and off we went into the car. She hooked me up to something she called a seat belt and we were off. We drove around and after about half an hour my Aunty shouted "Yay!" She said they found the scared dog and we could go home.

But we didn't go home, not right away. It had been an exciting day but there was more excitement to come. We went to visit a friend of hers and she came outside and they took me to a small yard and I got to sniff new smells and I even met another dog and we sniffed bums and bowed and jumped and it was fun!

Then we walked away and I thought, okay, time to go home. But we didn't go home. We went to another friend! This friend had good smells on their patio like food was going to happen. There was a man and a woman and each one told me I was handsome and beautiful and a good dog. Bowser Wowsers! Everyone thinks I'm a good dog. I'm pretty proud of that.

Well, there was food and I even got some steak! It was so yummy. I hadn't had my nap yet. I was pretty tired, so I decided they were nice people and I went to sleep. Again, like before, I was barely asleep and Aunty said it was time to go home. I met another dog in the parking lot and we play-bowed and sniffed and I got happier and happier. Then she said we had to go for real and we did.

That night I got to sleep on her bed for a little bit but then she put me in my cave. I cried a little, but not too much because I was too tired.

The next morning we got up early again, something about garbage day. That just means the loud big containers get put outside my territory and come back in later. I ran around the yard, did my business and then raced her! Boy was I fast. I went round the bush and back and up the stairs in no time at all. It felt good to run free. But I still had that leash attached to me, but no cone so life is good.

We went back in and Aunty showed me this dead thing and squeaked it. I jumped on the bed and she waved it in front of my face and squeaked it again. It was a little scary but she let me chew on it and I couldn't get it to squeak so I went to sleep.

As usual, the spellcaster woke me up, but it was not pleasant. I opened my eyes and then she squeezed the dead thing and it made such a racket I jumped up in the air and fell off the bed! Aunty laughed but there was no way I was getting back up there. I will attack the squeaky thing another day.

We went back outside for a pee then back inside and ate and then I had a nap while she talked to someone on the light thing that makes tippy-tappy noises.

I thought today was going to be relaxed after such an exciting weekend. Boy was I wrong. Aunty said she couldn't sit any longer and asked if I wanted to go for a walk. I said sure, why not. I even let her put the halter back on me. We went outside my territory, which was scary at first. Then we saw a man sitting in a chair in his garage and we went over. He had such great energy, like warm hugs and such, but he didn't look like he felt. He was a big man and I was a bit scared at first. Finally, I went near and it was okay so Aunty put me on his lap.

Oh my dawg this people's hands worked magic. I didn't know him but in about twenty seconds he'd massaged all the doubt out of me and I was almost asleep. My Aunty called him a dog whisperer. After a bit, Aunty said we needed to walk and smell the other smells.

We went to the big red thing, Aunty calls it a fire hydrant. Well, the smells were okay but they were all blurred together so we walked up the street and around. A house dog barked at us and asked me where I was going. I boofed back and said, "I don't know but look at me! I don't have a cone!"

We walked back to the nice man and I sat on his lap again. Aunty said she was very proud of me. Then a lady came out and I sniffed her and let her touch me too. I was almost asleep and then I spotted her.

By the curl of my tail, she was the prettiest thing I'd seen in a long time. They said her name was Becky and she was a Maltese, whatever that is. We sniffed each other silly and then she walked away. I was heartbroken. Maybe it's because of my ouchie, I don't know. But it was fun while it lasted.

Becky left with her guardian and then I saw another dog. This one looked just like me, but the opposite. She was big and black and curly-haired. Aunty told me her name was Daisy and she was a standard poodle, again, whatever that is. Well, Daisy took one look at me and ran from half a block away to see me.

We sniffed and boofed and sniffed some more and bowed and it was such fun. I was a little scared because she was big but had great energy.

There seems to be a lot of that just outside my territory. Then my Aunty said she had to get back to work, so off we went.

We had lunch and after she worked a bit she asked if I wanted to go outside again. The nice lady who was with the dog whisperer came over and talked to my Aunty. As she was leaving and we went to say goodbye, another lady waved and guess who she had with her. Another dog! I love the outside of my territory. Then Aunty invited them over.

I must admit I felt like this might be heaven or something. This lady dog, her name was Lexie, was gorgeous! My Aunty even took off my leash. She said I was a good boy and I always came when I was called in the yard so I didn't need it anymore. Oh, the freedom. I did zoomies to celebrate.

I was so happy to meet Lexie. She's older and something called a puggle and she looks like a potato, but she was so nice. For a round girl that Lexie could move! We ran around the yard lots and boofed and bowed and raced.

Once we were back inside and she sat in front of the tippy-tappy thing, something inside me changed again. I went up to my Aunty and asked if I could sit on her lap. She even picked me up.

I snuggled into her and she put kisses all over my head and I felt the sparky thing. I was safe! I can trust this two-legged and the other two-leggeds I met over the weekend and today. It's such a relief. After a few more pats, scritches and more kisses she said it was hard typing with me on her lap so she put me down.

It's dinner time now, so I'm going to go. I wonder what new things I'll experience tomorrow. And Happy International Dog Day everyone!

Until then,
Simon (Lonnie) The Timid Warrior

Be the person your dog thinks you are.

J.W. Stephens

Sprite

I can only tell you a part of my story. I don't know where I was and how I ended up in a high-kill shelter, but I can tell you it was horrible. One hundred percent awful. Then, some people came and took some of us away.

The ride wasn't too bad. I got to hang out with lots of other dogs. Most of them were older than me. I think I'm about a year old, maybe two, but I can't remember. I'm all black and the lady that picked me up at the shelter said she had to take me because black dogs don't get adopted very much. I don't know why. Maybe it's because you can't see us in the dark? Humans are so strange sometimes.

I remember getting to this big parking lot thing and lots of people were around. I just stayed in my cage, it was okay because I had a pee break a couple of hours before, and they fed me too. Then after two whole vanloads of dogs were taken away by other humans, it was my turn. My human was in a hurry. She said she had a sad dog at home who didn't like being left alone. Well as soon as those words happened, things moved fast. I got a collar and a kennel and food and a blanket and whoosh I was in her car and headed to somewhere.

We got to her place and she let me out to pee and introduced me to Simon. He was a nice dog. I sniffed his butt and other spots and I could tell he didn't have his bits anymore. I still have mine. I hope no one takes them.

The nice lady told me I was only there overnight because I had a new foster-to-adopt mom coming to get me the next day after work. I had no idea what that meant, but it sounded good.

The next morning I was rushed outside so I could do my piddle and piddle I did. I like having this other dog around. We bow-played and then barked and did pee wars. I ran out of pee so I think he won.

There's one thing you need to know about me and that is that I love hugs and cuddles. I want nothing more than to put my head under someone's chin and fall asleep there. Humans, the ones I've met lately, are really nice and I feel safe with them. I didn't feel safe before when I was on the street.

Even the humans at the shelter were nice to me. They said I was a cuddle-bug and they wanted to help me get adopted. They gave me a nice bath and then they cut my hair and gave me a mohawk! I thought it looked good. Then one of them decided to colour my white patch, blue. She said it would make me stand out.

So here I am in a different country, not looking like myself, with a radical haircut and a blue stripe down my front. I think it makes me look cranky, but people said I looked cute. I feel like I was just on one of those makeover shows.

The human that Simon calls Spellcaster is nice. She lets me snuggle up next to her and everything. She said that since it was a Sunday, we could spend most of the day outside, and so we did!

I got to chase butterflies and birds and played with Simon a lot. We even went for a little walk together. I met the neighbour lady too. I went right up to her, climbed in her lap and put my head under her chin. I like doing that. It makes humans soften up a bit. I heard her tell the spellcaster that I was spoken for and my person would be by later. She let me go and I went back into the yard.

After a long day of eating, chasing, zoomies and sleeping, another lady came over.

The spellcaster person told me that was my new mam, my forever protector. I liked that, but I was comfy so I just sat beside her and got more cuddles. After a bit, the spellcaster picked me up and handed me to the mam lady. I have a mam, a mammy. I feel pretty lucky. I hope she doesn't mind that I call her Mam. I snuggled right in under her chin and I felt her love gush out of her. Boy did I ever get lucky with this one.

I hope the lady next door doesn't mind. I liked her too, but she had cats, so I wasn't going to live there.

I wish I could tell you that everything was perfect after that. It was, but it wasn't. You see, Mam lives in a condo and I cry and bark when I'm left alone. We're working on it. I'm sure you, dear reader, are familiar with the drill. Short sections of time at first. Put the kennel in the bedroom so I can hear my Mam snore. Don't forget the blanket over the kennel to make it more cave-like.

I know Mam loves me already so I'm working hard to be quiet when she goes to work. I'm pretty sure if I can do that, we are going to have a great life together.

Sprite,
With the Mohawk

Dogs do speak, but only to those who know how to listen.

Orhan Pamuk

Simon (Lonnie) the Timid Warrior: Part 2

Days 19 and 20

It's been almost three weeks since I've been in captivity and I must say it hasn't been all bad. I've met some great dogs and some people who were pretty nice too.

Aunty says it takes three weeks for a rescue dog to destress and let their guard down so they can just be the doggos they were meant to be. She also said it would take three months for me to fully get acclimatized to my new life. Whatever that means.

She said in a few weeks I might be ready for adoption and that a nice person or family would love to have me in their home. Well, I kind of like her, and I don't want to go. She's pretty nice.

I love my yard. I've been doing zoomies for the past few days and I'm getting pretty fast. Aunty says you can see a small track in the lawn from where I've been running. It is so much fun!

But I do have a complaint. It's the spellcaster. As you may recall, a few days ago I wrote about the squeaky thing. She squeaked it when I was on the bed and I fell off the bed. I was so humiliated. Well, I've taken that squeaker dead thing and moved it so it's not near me and now and then I give it a good bite. Still, I can't make it squeak.

Back to my complaint. I don't like the bed thing. It doesn't make sense. I didn't go back on it for a day or two because, well, it bucked me off last time and I ended up on the soft floor.

Last night I decided I wanted scritches and rubs while the spellcaster read her book of spells. I hopped back up and got comfy. After a few scritches I went to lie at the end of the bed. I stretched out, feeling so relaxed, and BOOM! I was on the floor. I'm sure the spellcaster had something to do with it.

I just sat on the floor in front of the portal with the other dog in it that looked like me. It still didn't smell or bark or anything. I pleaded with my eyes for it to give me some answers, but he was silent. Sometimes I can see the spellcaster in it too. This is simply another reason to call her a spellcaster because it's nothing I've ever experienced before so it must be magick.

Right, back to the spellcaster. She laughed! I was confused and humiliated. Why would she do that to me? I wanted to be near her but she magicked me right off the bed.

I was pretty upset. So upset that I didn't tell her I needed to go outside to potty. Instead, I pooped in my cave as soon as the lights went out. I thought that would teach her, and I did have to go but being magicked off the bed made me forget, so I didn't ask.

She turned the light back on, looked inside, and said, "Oh, Simon. That one stinks." But it worked. She let me out of my cave and she said something about midnight as she flicked my poop into the yard. I came back in after another pee and watched as she put my poopy blanket in the wash and turned it on.

One would think after that, she'd let me sleep where I wanted to. But oh no! She got a couple of towels and put them in my cave and put me back in there. I was not amused and I did cry. And, just to get back at her I got up at six in the morning and started whining.

She let me out but she didn't come in the yard with me. She just stood on the deck and watched and yawned.

Which reminds me. I recounted and I think there are seventy big stones around the flower gardens. It's rained a bit, and I've had a few doggy guests, so now I have to start all over again and pee on each one.

A warrior's work is never done.

Until then,
Simon (Lonnie) The Timid Warrior

Days 21 to 23

Aunty says it's been three weeks since I moved in. It feels longer, but shorter too. I do love her pats and snuggles, but she's mean and puts me in my cave at night.

She says it is for my protection. What do I need to be protected from? I am a warrior. Sure I am a bit timid, but a warrior, nonetheless.

She says it's because I appear to lack depth perception when it comes to beds. Well, it's not my fault I forgot where I was.

For the past two days, I've been magicked off the bed onto the soft floor at least three times. Every time, she laughs!

I think she's an okay human, then she shows me how mean she is. Why, oh why, does she spellcast me off the bed? This time I thought she took a picture of me falling. She said she missed it because I'd fallen by the time she found the camera. So I ask you Diary, why is she more interested in taking a picture of me falling off the bed, than saving me from falling off the bed? Yes, I think you think what I think. She's a little bit mean, yep, she is.

Her friend said Aunty should put pool noodles under the bottom sheet, to form a bit of a barrier, but we don't have a pool and noodles are pretty small.

Now, remember earlier this week, I told you I had a guest sleep over. Well, that was Sprite. He was kinda nice, and he didn't get in my face too much and we only did the pee vs. pee thing a couple of times before another aunty came and took him away.

Well, shave my tail and call me a possum! She did it again. Some other two-legged showed up and left this, this, upstart pup with us! Aunty said it was only for two nights because she had family stuff and it was the long weekend.

I thought I could do two nights. After all, Sprite was a fine guest. Never in my face, always polite, always asked to be picked up, and never sat in my spot. He was a good houseguest and only peed inside once.

But this, this, Wylie guy, oh my dog! Here's what went down.

He got here and Aunty set up a small cave opposite mine in the sleeping room. There's lots of room, so I didn't mind.

We went into the house and this long-legged mischief maker started peeing on my Aunty's stuff. Well, I would have none of that! I lifted my leg and peed on the biggest chair in the big room.

Aunty told me to stop but I didn't. I had to show Wylie this was MY house. I realized I upset her when she looked at me and shook her head.

She said, "Simon, I'm very disappointed in you," then she went and got a wet rag and soap. Holy dental sticks—that actually hurt me. She was disappointed in me. But I was a good boy, wasn't I? She gave me a scruffle around my neck after that and said it was okay, I was learning, but I still felt bad.

It was that Wylie guy. It was all his fault. Right, I was telling you about him. Aunty made us go outside. It was fun at first. I peed, and he peed, on the tree, on the bush, around the side, and by the other tree. I thought, well, maybe he's not so bad. Then it happened.

Yes, you know what I'm talking about. Puppy energy in the face! Aunty says he's got the legs and the speed of a whippet but the face of a terrier. I don't care about that, just stay out of MY face.

I don't mind a butt and belly sniff. I don't mind pee games, and I'm always up for a good race. But get in my face, and wowzers, I get mad. I told him too. I told him by the back gate. I told him on the deck. I told him in the flower bed. (Aunty didn't like us in there.) But he would not listen!

I gathered up all my warrior strength, turned on him, and growl-barked "Get away!" He didn't. Like I said before: upstart. Yeah, I don't know where I get these words, but it means he's a youngster who takes advantage of being cute, or something like that.

Aunty put a wrap around his belly and we went in to eat. He tried to eat my food! Eat your own stuff giraffe legs!

Honestly Diary, I didn't know how long I could take his insolence.

That night, we sat on the deck and Aunty asked me up on the little couch. There we were, loving each other lots, and furry stork boy jumped up on the other side and she loved him up too! I rolled my eyes and sighed and just let it be.

At bedtime, I got to snuggle on the bed for a bit and Upstart McLonglegs went into his cave. Sure enough, there I was, all cozy, a smile on my face and BOOM! On the floor. She put me in my cave and I woke her up at six in the morning because, well, why not?

The next day was okay. We spent the morning outside and then Aunty put another diaper thing on Wylie and we spent the afternoon inside by the light thing that makes tippy tappy noises when she sits at it. She told me it was an office. I didn't care, there was a soft blanket and

I needed the sleep!

Every time we went outside the upstart got his diaper off and then annoyed me to bits chasing me and interrupting my private pee time. Aunty says he is just a youngster and it's okay that I teach him manners but not to hurt him. I tried and I think he got a bit better, but not much.

We stayed on the deck until way past dark after we had dinner. Aunty was running low on belly band things so we stayed outside so Wylie didn't pee on stuff inside. He curled up beside Aunty on the left and I did the same on the right.

At one point our noses met on her lap, but I was so tired I didn't care. I looked at this sassy pup closely though. His eyes were almost closed, but I could see all that bouncing and trying to play was just him trying to make a friend.

I guess he's not that bad. I have friends here, so I guess I could be nice, but only if he is.

Aunty said we have to find something good in all the moments we have because we never know how many moments we get.

Then she showed me a picture of someone called Miss Potato. Aunty said she got sick and had to cross the rainbow bridge.

She said all the people who tried to help her, the ones who helped me and all the other rescues, were sad because they couldn't save her. Aunty's face got a little wet, so I kissed it to make her feel better. She smiled and scruffled my neck again. I'm glad I helped. It was a good thing in a sad moment.

This morning, we all got up early and explored the yard. He was a bit better and at one point we just stood and wagged tails at each other. We even played a little.

I asked him if he was scared, and he said he was a little scared but some human told him that now that he was in the Okanagan he was going to be safe and he'd find a forever home and his people soon. That was nice to hear.

I wonder if Aunty is my forever home. I hope so, but she keeps telling me she's going on a trip and I can't come. But I don't want another home. I like this one.

After a few rounds of "Guess which rock I peed on," the lady who smelled like patience came in and talked to Aunty. I remembered her trying to put the collar on me a few weeks ago and I was so horrible to her.

Well, in my defence, I was scared. I gave her a few sniffs and even let her touch me. She's not so bad after all. I even ran around the yard with Wylie to show her how far I'd come in three weeks.

Before I knew it, they were gone and it was just me and the spellcaster. Yes, I'm back to calling her that.

She took a really tasty treat and tossed it into my cave. I, of course, followed it and she shut the door! She said something about brunch and family and weddings and a guest coming to stay soon and then she left.

She's back now, and we had a good snuggle on the outside couch and then another five-minute snuggle on the bed. She said I couldn't get too comfy or I'd fall off. Now we're back in the room she calls an office.

As for me, I found a few spots where Wylie peed in the house, and I peed on top of them. I don't think she noticed.

I just want some peace now because of the human guest coming soon. I'll keep you posted.

Until then,
Simon (Lonnie) The Timid Warrior

The greatest pleasure of a dog is that you may make a fool of yourself with him, and not only will he not scold you, but he will make a fool of himself, too.
Samuel Butler

Wylie

Hi there! My name is Wylie, or that's what they are calling me. I don't look like Wylie Coyote or anything like that, and I'm sure a lot smarter than him. This is the first part of my journey and I'm pretty amped to tell you about it.

When I was in California I had this wild haircut, I looked a little mad, like that Einstein guy. But the nice people at the shelter cut my hair for me and I think I look rather smol. In case you haven't guessed yet, I'm a young pup, not even a year old, but I'm smart!

So here's my hot take on what happened.

I get put in a van after being in this extra place, I mean dogs everywhere. No cap, the people were nice so that was a good thing. A couple of days and lots of pee breaks later, I got to this other place and this nice lady picked me up. She took me home and there were two other dogs there so I had a squad, very dope.

Then after a week, my new foster mom said she was going away for a little bit and I couldn't go with her. I was okay with that because this has been such a great adventure! She brought me to this other house with another dog. It was lit. I sniffed and ran and played but this other dog, I think his name was Simon, got tired of me after a bit. He was acting like an old man and I know he's not that old. At one point I was trying to play and he growled and barked and told me to go away. Okay boomer, be that way.

I knew I was there for the long weekend so that salty dog would have to get used to it. I know I'm riz. I mean who could resist? The new person certainly couldn't.

Then there was the other thing. Apparently, in this new place and at my other place, you don't pee inside. Well gyat, (can I say that here?) I peed everywhere before I got my hair cut off. Oh well, I don't care. The lady put a belly thing on me and I still got to lift my leg inside, but it didn't get on anything. Or so she thought. I peed on the back of her big round chair. I don't think she found it. I think the old dawg did though.

Well, that's pretty much how it went for three days. I'd try and play with the opps but he was only good for about ten minutes and then he got upset.

Bedtime was great. The new person put my kennel in her room and the Simon dog went in his and I got to stare at him and send him lovey eyes, even though he doesn't really deserve them. But like I said before. Too bad. I'm outta that crazy place, and this place has a yard and good food and nice people, so he will have to just get used to me.

At night, before bedtime, the new person sits outside on a raised thing, she calls it a love seat. After I run around and sniff everything, I jump up and let her pet me. I like her pets. They feel good like my original foster mama. I wonder where she is. Doesn't matter. She said she'd come back and I know she will.

After a few days of running around and good food, I think the Simon dog started to like me. After a really busy second day, we sat on that loveseat and I lifted my head and put it on the person's lap. Simon did the same from the other side and we almost touched noses. We just looked into each other's eyes and I swear I saw him start to like me.

Yes, I know he was calling me names like giraffe legs and once I even think he called me stilt boy. He's probably jealous 'cause he hardly has any height at all with those shorty legs of his. The new lady thinks I'm part greyhound or whippet because of how much I run and how fast I go. Truth is, I don't know, and I don't care.

I'm here now, and all I want is to be loved, love back, play, and eat and sleep. It's not complicated.

We were sitting on the deck after dinner and I heard another voice that sounded familiar. It was the blonde lady from when I first got here. Simon told me she's called an adoption coordinator, whatever that is. I was happy to see her and she told me I could have another sleepover at another different place. I wonder where my original foster mamma is. I think I love her already. I've been to so many homes in a few weeks, but each one is fun and has nice people, but still, I like the original one.

Sure enough a few days later, after playing and getting to know stuff at a new place, my original foster came back and took me home. I got to play with my new pack and I was so happy.

Every house I was at told me I was a good dog and no one was going to hurt me or abandon me again. I like that.

If you see a long-legged, black-and-white terrier/whippet-looking dog bouncing around, it might be me. I won't have the same name though because my original foster already had a dog called Wylie. She calls me Paxton. And just in case you were wondering, yes, I'm adopted now. My original foster mom is what they call a foster fail. I don't see how it's a failure if I get to live with her forever.

Stay chill.

Paxton (formerly Wylie),
Now in a Pack

When you adopt a dog, you have a lot of very good days and one very bad day.

W. Bruce Cameron

Simon (Lonnie) the Timid Warrior: Part 3

Day 24

I had to sneak in between all the going-outs and visits and guest stuff to write this, so it will be short. My spellcaster Aunty thought she was so smart yesterday. She tossed that treat into my cave.
But it gave me an idea. I didn't eat it, nope, I did not.

    At bedtime, she tried to put me in my cave but I said no, I'm hungry. I ran into the cave and ran right back out with my treat and jumped on the bed. She let me eat my treat and I was hoping she'd forget about me on the bed. She didn't. The good news is, I didn't fall off the bed, but she still remembered I was there.

Into the cave, I went. I waited patiently to hatch my super plan. I had the squirts a couple of nights ago cause of some soft beef food. Aunty took me off it and put me on chicken and I'm fine now, but it gave me an idea. It was dark and quiet and I could hear the spellcaster snoring. That's when I put my plan into action. I whimpered like I did when I had to poop twice before. She stayed asleep. I whimpered louder. She woke up. Bingo! I had her now.

She slowly got up and turned on the light. When she opened the cave I bounced right out of it and in one leap, I was on the bed. I was bow-playing and zigging and zagging, I was so excited to have fooled her. She shook her head and said, "Well you might as well go out," and out we went.

She turned the lights on outside and I zoomed and zigged and zagged and bounced all over the yard. Then she whispered/hollered at me. "Simon, go potty!" Yeah, she wasn't happy but she didn't feel angry either.

So I peed and went to my usual poop spot, but you know darn well I didn't have to poop. I ran back up the stairs, into the house, and up on her bed. She came in and tried to catch me to put me in my kennel. No way spellcaster. I'm playing the long game, you can't catch me. I'd zig and she'd zag. I'd bounce just as she pounced. It was such fun!

She sighed and said, "I'm too tired for this, let's wait until you calm down." She got into bed and patted the space beside her. She's done this before, gets me all comfy and calm, then scoops me up and deposits me in the sleeping cave. But, like I said, I had a plan. As she stroked my fur I closed my eyes and bore into her brain with the mind trick her rainbow bridge dog, Missy, taught me. I told her she was getting very sleepy, oh so sleepy.

It worked, her eyes closed and then fluttered open. Drat. It was time to pull out that which is irresistible. I rolled over (but not off the bed) and gave her my soft, bare, and vulnerable belly. Who could resist?

She gave me slow belly rubs and soon her hand stopped and I heard a small snore.

Success! I was on the bed and she was asleep. I knew I had to be quiet so I stayed very quiet, but not too close to the edge of the bed. She woke up in the morning and shook her head at me. "Oh, Simon, you are a sneaky boy," she said and then we got up. I think this is what some people call the dog training the person.

She got me back though. This afternoon she took me into the big bathing room and put me in the tub. I didn't like it but there was no way to get out. She says it's a soaker tub, perfect for doggos my size.

Suffice it to say, she got me. Not all of me, no, I'm not that easy. I let her wash the top of my head and ears, chest and body. No way she was washing my face and feet. Don't tell anyone but it kinda felt good, all that scrubbing.

Afterward, she wrapped me in a towel and dried me off. She'd shown me the dog brush earlier and I hated it so she let me smell her brush and used that. It's called a wet brush so it doesn't pull hair and I was okay with it. She said she has to wash it too now, but she doesn't care. And she cleaned my collar and halter. Then she sprayed some doggy perfume on me and took me outside.

It was great! I got the zoomies again and ran around and she sat on the deck with me and patted me and told me I was handsome and a good boy.

I guess that means I'm forgiven for casting my spell on the spellcaster. I hope it works again tonight. I have to go now, but I will write more later. She said the guest is coming tomorrow.

Until then,
Simon (Lonnie) The Timid Warrior

Days 25 and 26

If that was a long weekend, then I've now had one. It didn't feel much different except we moved around a lot. Around the house, around the yard, in the car, chairs outside, then home, and then another house, more car, it was exhausting.

Let me catch you up a little. So much to tell and the spellcaster needs the computer, so I'll be quick, kinda.

Aunty caved in, almost. She took my big cave and put it back in the office and put my bed on the floor in her sleeping room. She said if I could go the night without peeing in the house, and I was a good boy, I didn't have to be locked up. But if she went out in the day, I had to go into the cave. Fair enough. Well, she didn't have to tell me that twice. I was so good. (Shhh don't tell her I peed on the back of her big green chair. Well Wylie peed there and I had to cover up his smell.)

Anyway, I was up on the bed and I was careful and I didn't fall off. But it was just a short time, not at night time. Then she talked into some rectangle thing and said it was time to go.

We went to someplace called a winery and I sat on another lady's lap. She was nice and smelled like a dog, so she knew how to find my good ear-scratching spots. Then Aunty's guest arrived. She slept on my couch though and I had to jump up on Aunty's lap in the chair. I'm a good jumper but I prefer my couch.

Then we took the guest in the car and went for a drive. We got me more food and then went to Vernon to see another lady also called Aunty. There was someone named Uncle there too. I remembered this place. It was where I met the nice dog with great smells. He wasn't there but I met a new one named Quincy and they were very nice and we butt sniffed and bow played and then covered up pees. It was fun stuff. Aunty said I was doing very well on a leash, and I think I've got the hang of it now.

We were in the house and they were doing their human speak a lot so

I went to sleep. Then I heard a dog outside and I jumped up on the couch and onto my Aunty and watched the dog out the window. I wanted to go out but she said no. She sure knows how to spoil my fun. I never get to do anything alone. I'll show her, I'll escape one day.

The other Aunty said I was doing well because the last time she saw me, two weeks ago, I wouldn't let anyone touch me and I needed a leash on at all times. I wandered around her house and sniffed toes and got scritches from these nice people. It's better than being scared.

The rest of the weekend time went by quickly. We had visitors and I had to let Aunty know when the neighbours were outside. I chased robins and tried to figure out who was sleeping in Aunty's garden bed. Aunty even caught me trying to clean my face off after snuffling outside. She asked me if I was part cat. What a strange question!

Now, there were a lot of two-leggeds coming and going and then this morning, two more two-leggeds came and took the guest away.

Now, here's where I got the spellcaster's heart beating really fast. One of the two-leggeds left the gate open. Yes, you read that right. I was free! I wasn't sure what to do with my freedom, but I knew I had it. I was a warrior and I was out and I could do warrior stuff. The first thing I wanted to do was free all the other captive doggos that surrounded my territory.

I was only out maybe thirty seconds when I heard Aunty call me. The two-legged was calling too, but she told him to stop and not chase me because I would run away. She's pretty smart. I didn't know him, I would have run like crazy.

Instead, I heard these other doggos barking in their house so I went to the door to see if I could rescue them. Aunty was right behind me, using her spellcaster voice to get me to come but heck no, I was exploring! I ran to the next house, where my friend Lexie lives, but she wasn't there so I decided to make a break for it.

As I was running away I remembered the nice man with the big chair in the garage and I went and sniffed over there. Aunty was in hot pursuit but still talking sweetly. I knew what she was up to. No way was I going to give up my freedom. Besides, that male two-legged kept calling and Aunty finally told him to please hush. I heard another dog bark, and I was on my way to rescue it. This was it. I was free of my bonds, free to go wherever I wanted, free to rescue other doggos, and free to . . .

But I had to stop. The spellcaster lay down on the road, looked at me, and whimpered. Oh, my padded paws! I ran to her, hoping she was okay, but as soon as I got near she reached for me. Not this time spellcaster, nope, I'm outta here. I jumped away from her and smiled. This was a fun game. I didn't run away, I just stood far enough away that she couldn't touch me. I like this game.

She looked at me and shook her head. "Fine, be that way," she said and got up and dusted herself off. I didn't run, I just watched her because her energy changed. She went from calm words and a kinda worried voice to her don't care voice. Well, I need her to care, and I need her to care about me.

She told her guests to leave the gate open and to step aside. Then she looked at me and said, "C'mon Simon, that's enough. We have to go now." And she walked away from me. She turned around and said, "Well, are you coming or not?" and then she walked up the driveway to the gate.

If you've ever played hide-and-seek or keep-away, you know it's no fun if the other people stop playing. Then she turned around and said, "Well, come on then, let's go!" and she did it in her happy voice. So, I did what any good doggo would do, I followed her.

When I think back on my short journey into freedom, I realize it was the whimper when she was on the road that got me. I would have run like heck if she hadn't just got down on the road at my height. I guess, looking back, that was pretty smart because I forgot all about running away and rescuing other dogs.

Aunty says from now on, if she expects company, I have to wear my leash or she is just going to keep me in the house when her company is coming and going. She doesn't want another big heart flutter like the one I gave her today. I don't want to do that to her either, but it sure was nice exploring the neighbourhood on my own.

Until then,
Simon (Lonnie) The Timid Warrior

Days 27 to 29

TThings are going pretty well here in Warrior Land. It's been a little over four weeks since I came to this place. My Aunty Spellcaster has tried a few new spells this week, all of which, I might add, didn't work.

She went out a lot this week. Like every day. And except for earlier this week, which I already wrote about, she didn't take me. Why?

I'll tell you why. She doesn't think I'm a good enough hunter or warrior either. She goes out and comes back with food, but it's mostly for her. Where's mine? Oh right, in the pantry, never mind.

The first time she went out this week she tossed a Dentastick into my kennel in the office. I happily followed it in and then, WHAM! The jail gates slammed shut. I cried, "Why, why spellcaster, why you do this to Simon the somewhat still timid warrior? Why am I a prisoner? Have I displeased you? Have I not been a good boy?

She said I was a good boy and she had an appointment to get her back cracked. Whatever that means, it sounds like it would hurt. She did come back but I could hear her outside watering those trees. I whined and barked and howled. I sang her the song of my people, and it worked. She came inside and let me out. I fooled her though. I did a stinky mess over all three towels and it was all over my feet. Serves her right for locking me up. She says it was the beef again and I can't have any more beef dog food or people food. I don't care, I like the ones with chicken.

The next day, the same thing. She said she had an appointment.

She wouldn't tell me where. She took me outside for fifteen minutes, but I refused to poop. Pee, yes, all the time, all day long, but no poop. She'd even cleaned the towels that were in the kennel and tossed another treat in there. "Not a chance Spellcaster," I said, well, I barked and I ran away. She was not amused. She couldn't find the Dentastick either, 'cause I hid it outside by the tree. No, I won't tell you which one. You can't have it.

Well, she gave up, got me some doggy bacon treats and tossed them into the office. YUM! I ran after them and then, botheration, she did it again. She closed the baby gate to the office and left. I didn't cry as much this time, and I didn't have to poop, so I howled a bit and then went to sleep on the comfy blanket. No way I was going into the big jail cave.

Same thing the next day, only this time I brought the Dentastick back in the house after my morning surveillance of the grounds. She made me take it back outside because it was dirty. Yeesh, it was simply well-seasoned. I didn't fall for the treats this time and ran out of the office every time she came near. I've got your number spellcaster, if you can't catch me, you can't lock me up.

Then she did the thing I hate. She ignored me. She said, "Fine, be that way," and she sat down at the desk and made the tippy-tappy noises. I curled up beside her on the floor, as always. She got up, told me to stay, left, and shut the gate behind her. Well butter my butt and call me a biscuit. I fell for it again!

Now she says she's going out again today for girl time. I could use some girl time. I haven't seen my friend Lexie in three days. I miss my gorgeous older woman.

This morning Aunty was in the big space with the different smelling plants. She started pulling out the big ones with tiny spikey things on them. Then she got some big things out of the garden and took them into the house to clean. Well, she left this hand-shaped thing sitting out. It smelled like all of outside and a little bit of inside my Auntie's house too. I guarded it carefully, shook it a few times to make sure it was dead, and sat with my paw on it. Aunty came out and said I had to give it back. Spoilsport.

Oh, and there's the weird sounds she makes. Scares the heck out of me. We were lying on the bed last night, watching a show and this noise came from under the covers. Thunderation it was loud! I jumped really high and almost fell off the bed, but she caught me, which scared me even more. I may have given a less-than-warrior-like squeak and yip when it happened.

She said, "Sorry about that," and laughed. The spellcaster is always laughing, and I'm pretty sure it is at me. She said it was just a fart and that I did it too and mine smelled way worse. Confound it Spellcaster, my bum fluffs smell just fine thank you very much.

Anyway, what she won't tell you is this. I have been on the bed five whole nights in a row and I have not fallen off. In the morning, we even play on the bed and I zig and zag and we play bow and boof each other and I try to grab her hand with my teeth, gently of course. It is such good fun, and I never hurt her, but most important of all: I don't fall off the bed!

Aunty told me I might be ready to meet some new people and find a forever home soon. I love her and trust her, but it would be nice to be able to do that with the other two-leggeds. But they have to give me space to figure out if they are good or not.

She has some weird name for me now. I think it's my camouflage name. You know, for just in case we go on secret missions. When I go outside I get pretty excited and I kind of bounce when I run. Now she calls me Bouncy McFluffer. I kinda like it. Makes me smile.

Oh, and she found the pee. That was my mistake. It's been nice out so the windows have been open and I don't think she smelled the other little pees.

When she was working I snuck out into the living room and peed on the chair again, and it was a big pee. Well, she found it and spent a good half hour cleaning it. Now she watches my every move and won't let me wander around the house by myself.

I was just informed she needs the tippy tappy thing again, so I have to go. Pray for me and my impending incarceration this afternoon. I hope all will be well upon her return.

Until then,
Simon (Lonnie) The Timid Warrior

Days 30 to 34

Well, well well. Things have certainly been interesting again. Yes, I was incarcerated in the afternoon. But, true to her word, she came back in under three hours. I was not amused of course. She said she could hear me crying on the camera. I didn't know she was watching me that close!

But she did come back. I was a good boy and didn't pee or poop anywhere and I had great zoomies when we went outside afterwards.

The next day she said she was having a dinner party tomorrow and I needed to behave. Sure, I'm a good dog, that's easy. She spent an awful lot of time in the kitchen making great smells and she said it wasn't for me. I did get more soft food with my meal, so that was nice.

I went outside for a little bit and she was busy pulling plants from the side garden so I decided to help. I snuck through the back entrance to the food garden and started digging. The dirt was nice and soft from where she pulled up the prickly leaf plants. Boy was it ever fun! She saw me and boy oh boy did her voice get loud. She told me to "Stop digging in the garden!" Well hey spellcaster, you dig in here, why are you better than me? Huh? She got closer and she meant business so I jumped out and did zoomies and soon she was happy again. I think my zoomies make her smile.

That night she told me this Martingale collar was making my chest black because of the metal so she washed a couple of other collars and tried them on. I didn't like the little one, it felt funny and was too tight. However, my new bright blue collar with doggy prints on it fits perfectly!

She transferred my tags and cleaned my chest and wow, does it ever feel better. It's not as heavy. She said it's because I'm a good boy and mostly come when I'm called so I deserved a new collar. Then she added I still had to wear a harness or halter thingy when I go for walks, but that's okay.

In the morning we went out and explored the yard and I peed and she pulled more things she calls weeds. Then we came in and spent the morning in the office. At lunch time she got all weird and moved furniture around and told me I had to stay out of her way. What is this, stay out of her way stuff. I need to follow her everywhere, she knows this.

Well, there was the growly thing on the soft floor and then some smelly stuff that she wiped everywhere, and then the broom. She brought out this other thing and put water and smelly stuff in it and pushed it all over the floors where the furniture once was. I liked the smell and I followed her everywhere. She threatened to put me in my kennel, so I stood back and let her work. What a spoil sport! I think my paw prints look great on the floor.

Then there were more great smells. My spellcaster sure does cast good spells in the kitchen. I hope I get to taste some of them later.

Once she finished all her moving around I went outside to check for intruders. Sure enough, some lady came through my gate into my territory. I barked up a storm until Aunty came out. She said, "It's okay Simon, I see her," so I stopped barking and went into the house.

Pretty soon there were lots of people in the house and they all told me I was really cute. Aunty told them to just put their hand down and let me come to them. I did too. I smelled every hand. I could tell one lady really wanted to touch me so Aunty gave her some of the special treats.

I was excited, I could smell them and I remembered how good they tasted. Well, apparently, the lady didn't have her ears on because she ate them. She ate my treats! I went and got Aunty and told her. She asked the lady where the treats were and when she saw the lady chewing Aunty burst out laughing and told the other lady they were my treats.

This lady ran to the sink and spat everything out. She didn't even spit it over to me. How rude. I watched as she rinsed her mouth out a few times with the water from the sink. Serves her right for eating my treats.

After everyone ate I got a small taste of the zucchini and it was so yummy. Then they all sat around and talked. Sometimes it got cranky, but then it was nice, and then sad, then really happy. They talked about a lot of things.

When it started getting dark some people left and others sat on the deck with us. I really liked it. So many in the pack. So many pats and scratches for the taking if I wanted them. Then, poof! They all left and it was just me and the spellcaster.

A few hours and a walk around the yard later, it was time for bed, but I wasn't ready for that. No sirree bobba-runie. I was still kind of excited by all the people, and I was so proud that I didn't get scared of them. I felt something in my head click or burst or change or something. I jumped up on Aunty's bed, right onto her squishy bits and just grinned at her.

"See how happy I am!" I said, but I don't know if she understood. I didn't realize she had such a big pack and I liked them. I jumped off her squishy bits and onto the floor and back up on the bed. She told me it was time to sleep. I said, "Sure!" and jumped on her head. Then I tried to snuggle between the pillows, and then I ran to the end of the bed and then jumped on her squishy bits again.

"Simon! Stop that!" she said. But I didn't care. I was so happy that one of the fear bubbles in my brain was gone. I just wanted to be as close to her as possible. I snuggled up onto her squishy bits again and she lifted me and put me beside her. So I did what any good dog would do. I got busier than a squirrel in a bucket of nuts. I jumped off the bed and ran down the hall. Then I ran back and bounced back on the bed, right on her belly. I jumped off again, but she didn't chase me. I didn't care. I ran around and around and finally, she got up and asked if I was hungry. Of course I was! She fed me a little bit of kibble and I gobbled it up. Being happy makes me hungry. We went outside again, but I didn't pee.

When we got inside she crawled back into bed and I jumped on her again. Boy, this was such fun. I may have taken it a bit too far because I did this a few more times. Then she said, "I don't care, I'm going to sleep," and she rolled over and turned out the light.

I explored the house on my own, but I didn't pee or poop, just sniffed everywhere the people had been. They sure left an awful lot of smells in my house. Once I'd smelled them all I jumped back on the bed and sat on her head. She was not amused.

We went outside again, I think she said it was one in the morning, but it was just as dark as when we went to bed. I finally got her to let me sleep on the other side of the bed and then I woke her up at five because I had to pee. I guess I should have gone the other times I went out. She's a good spellcaster though, she got up and let me out to pee and then we went back to bed, again.

You know what? It was the funnest night ever. I just want to curl up to her and get pats and everything.

She wasn't very happy the next day. She said she was really tired. Well, go nap then! I did, but she did the tippy-tappy thing in the office for hours and hours. When she was done we watched some TV and went for playtime outside. And of course, she fed me again. I love it here and I just can't believe how happy I am. She didn't even run in the yard with me after dinner. Instead, she stood on the deck and cheered me on. I did zoomies for ten whole minutes. After all, I had to burn off all that extra food I had. She watched me when I pooped and said I was a good boy and then it was time for bed.

When we got into the sleeping room she said, "You'd better not do that again," and I just smiled. I didn't jump on her head but I love her squishy bits and I snuged in good. She just put me on the other side of her.

I woke up at five again and told her it was time to get up. She gave me a grumble and said, "I don't care, I'm tired." So I went into the big living space and found a spot by the front door and pooped. I've never pooped inside before, I hope that it was okay. Once I was done I felt great and jumped up and snuggled her on the wrong side again. She just muttered and moved aside. I am winning!

Okay, so this morning, when she got up, she found the poop. She just shook her head and told me not to do that anymore. She cleaned it up and put down a pee pad, she said, "for just in case." I don't know what that means.

We went outside this morning, but it was raining and we didn't stay out long. I had a yummy breakfast and I helped her with laundry. She left the spare room door open and since I'd just eaten, well, you know what I did. It was cold and wet outside, I didn't want to go out there. I know, I should have told her. She just sighed, picked up more poop, and said she was glad I didn't pee. Now the door is closed again. Darn it!

Now you're all caught up. Kinda. She said I am going to a meet and greet on Saturday and might meet my forever family. I don't understand forever, I only understand now, but I'll go if it makes her happy.

Until then,

Simon (Lonnie) the Timid Warrior

Days 35 and 36

My Aunty Spellcaster finally figured out why I was being so weird on the bed the last few days. I wasn't even sure why I was being weird, but together, we figured out the problem. She was getting pretty annoyed with me jumping on her side of the bed and up on her squishy bits. She even took off the blanket and washed it, just in case it was the blanket. Well, I can tell you, it wasn't the smell. I think I didn't like the way it felt, or maybe I liked it too much. I don't know.

Anyway, the reason I was being so weird at bedtime was the fleece-type blankets. It was odd the way it felt on my feet or my newly shaved belly area. It made me feel happy and weird all at once. She even put a different blanket on the bed, but I hated it. As soon as she moved it, I was happy to lie anywhere near her, but not on that darn blanket. Well, I would but only on her squishy bits. I'm so glad we figured that out!

We've been for more walks and I'm doing so well on the leash. Aunty says I'm a pro. And the neighbours give me treats when I go over to visit them. Oh, and I met a cat. Well, not really met. She was in a window inside and I was outside and I really wanted to see her but when my Aunty lifted me up, she hissed. The cat, not my Aunty. I got the hint. She didn't want to be friends.

Anyway, that was just a little update before the big news day.

I went to the meet and greet and there were so many people and dogs there! I met a nice couple outside who had a dog my size, but she was bossy. I might get to like her, but only time will tell. She snarled at me, so I don't know. Aunty said they might want me.

I didn't poop or pee outside when we got to the place. I was too excited by the new smells. As soon as we went into the Tail Blazers store to meet the people, I freaked out a bit. Not in a bark-my-face-off way, nope. I pooped. It's what I do when I'm nervous. Aunty helped clean it up and then a nice person came and cleaned up the rest.

Aunty led me to the big area and gadzooks, it was noisy. I tried to run away but she led me around the back of the aisles to get used to the noise. Then this dog was barking and came at me and I hid behind Aunty. Then the barky dog left. Phew, I didn't want to prove how tough I was.

We came around a corner and Aunty picked me up and as soon as she did all these people came over to me and tried to pet me and my eyes got all big and round and I begged Aunty to do something. I tried crawling up on her shoulder.

She's my hero because she told the people, no, please don't. She said it in the same voice she used with me sometimes. It's not loud, but it is firm. Then she explained I had to sniff first and then maybe they could touch me. I could feel the disappointment coming off this one lady. She super-duper wanted to touch my curly hair, but I was pretty timid feeling. I wasn't up for it, at least not yet. She was nice though, I liked her smell.

Aunty held me and answered questions and then we went to a quiet part of the room and she let me down. There was a big dog there that had no smell! Aunty said it was a statue or something but it sure looked real.

We spent the next hour meeting other dogs and people. She said that a lot of the people there were volunteers and dog foster folks. So many smells and doggos everywhere. Oh my, I was having a time! There was this one little girl, Doris, she was so sweet, but I could tell she was a bit timid like me. Then there was a wee little dog named Molly. I loved her energy! She was bouncy and fun and I just wanted to play but there were too many people. I met a young pup named Billy, he was okay but I had to snarl a bit to tell him to get out of my face. I don't like young boy dogs, nope, I do not. All that puppy energy is too much for me. I prefer my dogs, female, and mature. Aunty says if I was a human I'd make a good gigolo whatever that is. She said I already kinda was in my previous life because I was a stud.

Aunty picked me up again and we went and talked to more people but I think they wanted someone more like the bouncy gal, Molly. Or the impertinent pup, Billy. Aunty said not to worry. The patience lady, remember her, the blonde one, she would make sure I got a good forever home.

Yeah, I forgot to mention that I peed at the door. Aunty was disappointed but then the blonde patient lady cleaned it up. I think she's like a superhero or something. Aunty told me about all the dogs she finds homes for, how busy she is, and how she still has time for every doggo. I think she is a superhero. I think I finally understand who these people are. They are just trying to match up people with dogs so everyone is happy. I like that idea.

Then most of the people left and the dogs left and then I was minding my own business, sniffing away and this lady came over and touched me. I don't know why I let her but she had great hands. She knew just where to pat and scratch.

A few minutes later Aunty picked me up and put me in the lady's arms. She said that the lady was a dog whisperer and I would feel safe with her. Heavens to Murgatroyd, I did! We walked around the store and she was so nice to me.

I don't know if I met my forever person or people today. I kinda liked the lady and man with the bossy dog, but I don't know if they liked me. I could maybe like the bossy girl dog, as long as she didn't hurt me.

We are back at home now and Aunty has to get ready for something called happy hour. She said I get to come to and meet more neighbours. Aunty told me Lexie isn't back until tomorrow. I miss my dog friend. I do love older female dogs with spunk.

Aunty just told me I must be an old soul because I use so many old-timey words. I don't know what that means. After today, I'm exhausted! But I will write again next week.

Until then,
Simon (Lonnie) the Timid Warrior

Days 37 to 40
So many people! Aunty says I have to get socialized so I can go to a forever home. And I think that means she's going to let everybody pet me.

After the meet and greet, there was even more stuff to do. A nice lady came over for tea and talk and as soon as she left we went next door to the neighbours and I sat on the man's lap again. I even sat on a lady's lap and she was squishy like my Aunty. Just as I got comfy we had to go because another person came to visit Aunty. She sure is popular.

Finally, everyone was gone and I got my snuggles and had a good night's sleep.

The next day another lady came to visit us with her dog. I liked the dog and the lady was okay too. The people talked and had coffee and I got to run around with the other dog. She's just the kind I like, older than me and a girl. We had a great time. She wasn't bossy or anything.

At dinner time Aunty fed me and then she left me. I was a good boy and didn't bark or cry much when she was gone. I know she's coming home because she said she would.

The last few days have been pretty much the same. We get up in the morning and cuddle and then I go out and run around for a bit. Aunty sits at the light thing and does the tippy-tappy and every couple of hours she takes me outside.

Sometimes we go for a long walk, and sometimes just for a walk across the way to see the neighbours. They have treats, I like them. One morning my older puggle girlfriend Lexie came over and boy did we have fun in the yard. What can I say, I love older girl dogs.

Today she left me again in the morning to get more back cracks and I was good again. I don't pee anywhere except outside. Okay, I did pee on that spot on her chair where Sprite peed, but I had to get rid of the smell. Aunty put a pee pad over the top of it just in case it doesn't smell to my liking.

The little Maltese girl dog came to visit today and I was excited but just like the last time, she snubbed me. I don't know why she does that. I wanted to play. My aunty said that people and dogs are a lot alike. Sometimes you click with someone, and sometimes you don't.

I'm still a little scared of getting my halter on and of being picked up. I'm trying hard not to flinch or scream, but sometimes it still freaks me out.

A neighbour lady tried to pick me up today and I screamed and nipped at her. I didn't bite hard, just enough to let her know she shouldn't touch me.

Aunty said I'm doing great as I let a dozen people pat me and touch me this week without me getting scared.

Then she sat me down and told me some things. She said she had to go away for a long time and that she couldn't take me with her. I could feel the sads coming off of her.

She said if she could, she'd cancel her trip and keep me. But she can't because she made something called a promise to a lot of people. She told me I'm going to another foster home next week. I don't know if I like that idea. She said maybe we're like star-crossed buddies, that we just weren't meant to be this time. I don't understand that. I only know that I am safe with her.

She gave me another Dentastick and told me not to worry, that it would all work out as it should. I sure hope she's right. In the meantime, I'll just chew on this and enjoy her company.

Then Aunty just told me that the little girl dog I liked from the meet and greet, is coming over for a visit! Aunty's friend adopted her. (She wanted me at first, but I don't think I was a good fit for her condo.) Anyway, I'll finish up this chewy thing and then I get a play date!

Until then,
Simon (Lonnie) the Timid Warrior

Days 41 and 42

Hey everybody, wow have I been having fun! That Molly girl from the meet and greet came over to play. Her adoptive mom is so happy to have her and loves to watch us play together. We did zoomies for twenty minutes, rested for ten and did zoomies again for another twenty minutes. Aunty says she's never seen me this excited.

Oh! Oh! I broke my record. There was a foster dog called Rosie Posey who lived here with Aunty. Aunty told me she could make it from the tree to the back of the yard, around the bush and back to the tree in seven seconds. She dared me to do the same. Well, I did it! And I did it in seven seconds a week or so ago. But yesterday, I did it in SIX seconds. I am a speedy guy. You wouldn't know it to look at me, but I'm hecken' fast!

Then last night Molly's mom asked if Molly could come for a playdate again 'cause she was taking a class. Aunty said yes and I was so darn excited when Molly came over. We ran around the yard and peed everywhere and sniffed each other's bums. Then when it was dinner time for Aunty she brought us inside. Molly is really little, like more than half my size, but she's a toughie. She body-checked me at least a dozen times. She does this thing by jumping up in the air, spinning, and slamming into me. I wonder if she watches hockey.

Anyway, it's been a fun couple of days. Aunty's left me a few times, and I've barely barked, but I did have what she calls accidents. Seriously, it wasn't an accident, I was mad so I peed. Well okay, I wasn't mad, I was lonely and a little scared so I peed. But I bet if Molly had been here with me or another dog, I would have been okay.

Speaking of other dogs, my Aunty says there's a new place for me to go live where there are three other dogs that love to play. She says I'm going to like it there. I think I will, but I will miss my Aunty Spellcaster. She was a little sad at first because she has this epic journey she's going on and dogs can't come. She's happier now that she knows I'll have friends.

It's hard to believe that a month and a half or so ago I was so scared I wouldn't let anyone touch me. Now, I even let Aunty's friends pet me. I still get scared at loud noises and if Aunty sneezes or, well, you know the other thing, I still jump a little. I don't think I'm quite ready for a forever home yet. Maybe if they had a nice yard and a dog my size, that was nice, then I might be. For now, Aunty says she is going to snuggle me every chance she gets until I have to leave.

Until then,
Simon (Lonnie) the Timid Warrior.

Days 43 to 49

Aunty Spellcaster says this is it, my final days with her. I hope she knows how much I love her. I could lay on the bed staring into her eyes forever, as long as she keeps rubbing my tummy and chest and back and legs and ears and head . . . well you get the idea.

She gave me lots of good advice before I go to my next foster. She said that most foster people are spellcasters. They use nice, calm words and they will tell me when I've been a good boy and it will make me feel better.

These last few days have been wonderful. I'm getting extra pats and scritches and she sings to me every night. I like "You Are My Sunshine" and "Beautiful Boy," but my name isn't Sean so she says Simon. She made up a song for me too. She said it's like "Hush Little Baby," but she sings "Hush Little Doggy" and it has lots of stuff that rhymes. I don't completely understand it, but I like being sung to. Here's what she sings.

> *Hush, little pup, don't you fear,*
> *Aunty's song will bring you cheer.*
> *And if you're feeling all alone,*
> *You'll soon have a family of your own.*
> *In your new home, you'll have so much fun,*
> *With lots of toys and room to run.*
> *A new aunty will love you so,*
> *And take you out when you have to go.*
> *If accidents happen, she won't mind,*
> *She'll clean it up and be so kind.*
> *And if you wonder where I'll be,*
> *Just remember this song from me.*
> *Though we'll be miles apart,*
> *You'll always be in my heart.*

I like singing. I hope new people sing to me too. I'm still skittish, yes, I know this word now. I used to think she was calling me ticklish, but I'm not. She said that maybe that's just me, being skittish. She told me she had a girl dog who looked like me, but she's gone over the rainbow bridge. Her name was Maggie. Aunty said she didn't trust most people and she wasn't even a rescue. This Maggie dog only liked people she liked, if that makes sense. She liked the grandma and grandpa, and one of the sisters, one of the sisters' husbands and a great aunt and of course Aunty and her daughter. After a while, she got to like a cousin, but that was it. Aunty said she could count on two hands how many people she liked to be around. I guess that means it's okay if I don't like everyone right away.

Aunty said that she messaged the new lady and she's excited I'm coming. She even asked Aunty if she wanted updates on me. Aunty said yes, she sure did! I think that made her a little less sad.

She said that soon, once I get more settled and trusting, I'll go to yet another home. This one will be just right for me. She explained that the adoption coordinators go through all the applications and look for someone who is a good match. I hope they have a yard and another nice dog. I would like that.

Aunty told me that someday I might see her again. It could be at a beach or on a walk. She told me that foster people like her rarely get to see the dogs they foster after they go to their forever homes. I think that must be hard. Aunty's neighbour said she doesn't know how my aunty does it, bringing all these dogs into her life and then letting them go.

She told her it was hard and every time she cried just a little. All the people who foster dogs fall a little bit, and sometimes a lot, in love with us. That's what helps us become stronger and braver doggos. I think Aunty is right and that most fosters are spellcasters, and the spell they cast most often, is love.

They're here now, my new fosters. I like the smell of them, and I wagged my tail when I saw them. I like their energy. Aunty's energy feels weird though, like something inside broke just a little bit. I think it was a piece of her heart. I gazed into her eyes and gave her a piece of mine so she would be whole again. I think she has a lot of different dog hearts in her heart. I hope she feels better soon.

She cuddled me a lot on the outside couch and told me she loved me and to be a good boy. Of course, I'll be a good boy, I won't let you down.

I'm a little bit scared. My big cave and little cave, along with my soft stuff, my dead thing, and my food are in the new fosters' car. I guess this is it, what she was talking about.

They put me in my small cave and Aunty put her nose next to mine to say goodbye. I love you Aunty Spellcaster. I will be a good boy and I will never forget you. I stuck my tongue through the bars and gave her a kiss to take away some of the tears.

I don't know what my future will bring, but I do know that I've experienced unconditional, wonderful, love. I believe there's more out there for me.

I hope my story has helped you understand what us rescues go through and how we can become good and happy dogs despite our history. Aunty told me we're like people that way. Sometimes all you need is a safe place to land, some food, water, and love. Lots and lots of love.

Who knows, maybe I'll see you on a walk someday.

Until then,

Simon (Lonnie) the Timid Warrior

AUTHORS NOTE: Simon got adopted! He is on his final name now. No more Caution, no more Lonnie, and no more Simon. He is now Floyd and has a loving mom and dad and a cute doggy sister. We wish him all the best as he enjoys his best life.

The average dog is a nicer person than the average person.

Andy Rooney

Sedona

Pregnant, Sick and Scared

Hi. My name is Sedona and I've been through so much lately. I think it's important that you know what some of us dogs go through when we are rescued.

My life before was, well, let's just say it wasn't pleasant. I'm a pug, a two-year-old, girl pug. I left the shelter sick, pregnant and covered in mange/scabies. There were a lot of sick dogs in the shelter so I was just one of many.

When we finished our long car ride I was exhausted. I didn't even care what happened to me. There were lots of happy noises as other dogs went away with people, but I stayed in my travel cage. Then I saw a nice yellow-haired lady looking around and I saw her face when another family took the pug she thought she was getting. She was a bit disappointed but then they explained to her that sometimes they change fosters because a different dog might do better with them. That's how I came to live with her.

They opened my crate and I was so scared. I watched my first foster mama's face again and I thought she was going to cry. I didn't know why. I knew I felt bad, but did I look that bad too?

I was trembling when they took me out of the crate and I was pretty weak. Not from the trip, they fed me along the way, but I didn't eat much before that. The yellow-haired lady looked me over and asked if I was pregnant. Yes, I was, as I had been so many times in the past. My skin itched all over, and I knew I had patches where all my fur fell out. I heard someone say it was probably mange, like scabies for humans. After some talking and getting a collar, leash, food, a bed and a clean crate, off I went into her car.

When we got to her house, I was still pretty scared. They showed me something called stairs and I was to climb up them to get into something called a house. Well, I finally made it up the stairs and went inside. I am not ashamed to tell you, I thought I was going to die there.

Then something fabulous happened. This yellow-haired lady, my first foster mama ever, had other pugs in the house! I was so happy I even wagged my tail. They were really nice to me, both the humans and the other dogs.

I loved it there and I learned very quickly that if I wagged my patchy tail and went up to the humans they would hug me and pat me. It was heaven! I'd never been touched like that before by humans.

They took me to the dog doctor and I think he said I had sarcoptic mange. That's what happens when dogs live in unsanitary conditions. As I said, life before wasn't pleasant.

The dog doctor gave my first foster mama some medicine to help stop the itching and maybe even get some hair back. She said I had to have a bath every day, but I didn't mind because I was so tired of feeling filthy.

The dog doctor also said that I was pregnant with six little wee ones in me and I would give birth in a week or two.

My foster mama took me home, bathed me and fed me the bestest tasting food ever. I had a hard time eating at first so she fed me with a syringe. She said I needed to fatten up before I became a mama. I already love my foster mama, she is the best!

I was doing pretty well and loved my baths and food, but then I started having trouble breathing and I got a snotty nose. We went right back to the dog doctor and I got some medicine. He said I was pretty run down from my before life, and the mange and the pregnancy. It was good that we caught it in time.

Unfortunately, I got worse when we got home. My first foster mama (FFM) stayed up with me most of the night in the steam of the shower room. She even held me upright so I could breathe easier. She patted and loved me, cleaning out the snot from my nose and goop from my eyes. I could tell she was tired, but she stuck it out with me. She's a great foster mama and after a couple of days, I started to feel better.

I loved living with my FFM and her other pugs, but she told me I had to go to another foster mama when it came time for me to give birth to my babies. I didn't like that because she's my best friend, but I have to do what she says. She's something called a nurse and she has to go back to work and look after sick people now and can't be with me all the time. With me being pregnant and all, the Paws It Forward people decided I should go somewhere else. But, I got to stay with her for ten whole days and it was, up until that point, the best ten days of my life. I really love my FFM. I hope I get to see her again.

When I got to my second foster mom's (SFM) house I was scared. She was nice though, and she had nice people living with her. FFM told me that SFM had lots of experience with puppies being born, so I felt a little bit better, but I was still wary of them.

Even though it is nice here, I keep looking up, hoping to see my FFM. She was so nice to me and I want her to meet my pups when they come.

I'm still contagious so my SFM sleeps with me in the spare bed in her home office. It's my room now.

I saw the same look on SFM's face as I did on FFM's face when she first saw me. Am I really in that bad shape? I know I don't feel good, but is it that bad?

My nose is still running with yellow gunk and my eyes are leaking green mucus down my face. My cough is not as bad but now I have a hack. I'm still pretty itchy because of the mange and little black specs of skin appear everywhere I travel. My SFM says I can't move around much because I am super contagious.

They made me a nice bed too. They call it a whelping pen and they set it up with nice soft towels and a metal kennel with puffy blankets. I am lucky because I can walk around the office freely. It's a much bigger space than where I was before, you know before they came and rescued me. My SFM put a humidifier in the office to help me fight my infection.

I was all settled in nicely and then SFM said I had to go back to the dog hospital, that it's an emergency. Heck, I don't care. I just want to sleep and car rides are kind of interesting. We got there and the dog doc explained that I was brachycephalic, which means my skull is short and I have a pushed-in nose. Well of course I do! I'm a pug. But he said there was more going on with me than pregnancy, mange, and pneumonia. I also had an eye infection.

I had so many medicines! I had to get drops in my eyes and shampooed every couple of days plus the other medication for worms and such. I'm so lucky that people donate to organizations like Paws It Forward. If they didn't, the dog doctors and fosters wouldn't be able to help me.

My SFM couldn't believe how skinny I was, despite being very pregnant. You could see my hip bones and ribs. They decided to fix that and put me on an expensive, high-calorie, gastro dog food, both soft and hard.

Just when I thought things were going to get better I had to also take probiotics because I had bad diarrhea. They also told my SFM I have a mild heart murmur. Geeze, what else could go wrong with me!

The next few days were uncomfortable what with the itching and the snot and such, but it got better. I still itched, but not as much and the yellow goop stopped coming out of me. I think the humidifier helped.

I don't want to complain, because I'm not a complainer, but I find it hard to eat. I just don't care that much. My SFM went out and got me some organic bone broth and mixed it with my special food. I like it a lot. You would think being so skinny I wouldn't be fussy, but I am. I don't know this food, it's just not what I'm used to.

Happy Birthing Day

One day my bestie, my FFM, came over with a case of good dog food. I heard her voice just as I felt a twinge in my belly. Could this be it? Was I in labour? I couldn't tell her what I was feeling and she gave me a head scratch and then she left. As soon as she left, my labour became really noticeable. My SFM raced to me and told me my foster dad had gone outside to stop my FFM, my bestie, from getting away. She came running back into my room and I was so happy to see her. I had my FFM and my SFM and my foster dad nearby so I wasn't as scared as I would be if I was alone.

My first puppy was born around 6:30 pm with no difficulty. My second puppy came right after and puppy three came twenty minutes later. I was so tired I could hardly clean them. But that was okay because SFM dried off my puppies for me and stimulated them.

I had to get moving to get these pups out so I walked around in circles and my foster moms made sure I didn't squish my newborns.

After a bit more time out popped puppies four and five. I was exhausted, I just wanted to sleep. My foster moms told me all the pups were an average size and healthy. We waited another half an hour and finally, my last puppy was born. Puppy Six was not like the others. I tried so hard but I was too weak and couldn't get the amniotic sack off this new puppy. My SFM jumped right in and opened the sac for me.

It was gross, it was full of green goop and my puppy was having trouble breathing. My SFM was amazing. Without hesitating she sucked the mucus out of it. My foster moms worked together using some weird contraption to suck more mucous out while the other massaged my little one.

There was a lot of talk and then it was decided I needed to get to the dog hospital again. We all fit into a laundry basket and off we went. I heard them talking and they said just in case the little one doesn't make it, they should name it. They called him Mouse because he is so small compared to my other pups. All my other pups were girls.

When we got to the dog hospital they took little Mouse away. He was so cold compared to the other pups. They warmed him up and came back and told my foster moms that he probably breathed in the goop in the sac. They cleaned him out properly and in a few hours, he was ready to come home with us.

My bestie FFM had to go home to her family and I was left with my SFM. She's good to me, and I think I love her too. She sleeps in the office and checks on my puppies all the time and helps Mouse to latch on. Most of my pups weigh almost seven ounces but little Mouse only weighs three ounces.

Mommy Time

I didn't get a lot of sleep over the next few days and neither did my SFM. She's so good to me. I can't believe how things have changed in a little over two weeks. From a crowded animal shelter to a comfy home. I am lucky to even be alive.

My SFM spoils me. She put up a nanny cam to watch me when she wasn't there and she put in a nice heater to keep me and the pups at just the right temperature. Did you know puppies cannot generate their body heat? The heat in the room must be perfect for them.

My little Mouse and I still need the humidifier. He's on an antibiotic two times a day for the next seven days . My foster has to help little Mouse latch, especially before and after giving the oral antibiotic. She also helps some of the other smaller pups latch on.

As for me, I'm getting healthier and I'm so glad too. Unfortunately, it's going to be a bit longer before my scabies, eye infection and upper respiratory infection are gone. I still get antibiotics twice a day as well as my medicated shampoo and I get Revolution every fourteen days. I still get eye drops and I have a dewormer to take every thirty days. My dog doctor says he'll take a closer look at my heart when I'm stronger.

I bet you're wondering what has to be done to keep me on the road to health. Well, let me tell you my SFM is amazing. I am contagious so she had to change my bedding all the time. She would take it all out, wipe it down, vacuum and do laundry. Then she puts back all new bedding for me and my babies. She is always washing the floor too, just in case. This foster mama and dad even made me a special area outside that's fenced off and away from their dogs. That's a lot of work.

I like their other dogs too. Venice is a foster fail. (That's what they call it when a dog gets fostered and never goes to another home. Not a failure though, more like a win for everyone!) Anyway, there's a puppy, Venice, from another California dog, Elma. Elma was thrown out of a car window along with another pug, Caesar. Thankfully, someone saw and picked them up. They ended up in a shelter in San Bernardino County, California. The same shelter I ended up in. Pregnant Elma ended up being fostered by my SFM as well and she kept her pup, that's Venice.

Pups Are a Week Old

Mouse has finished off the last of his antibiotics and he's even gained a few ounces. He's still smaller than the others, but he's growing. My foster family helps with everyone chipping in and caring for me and my puppies.

I also found out that it's not just my new foster family and my first foster who are making sure I'm okay. My SFM told me three coordinators were making sure I had the right food, medicine and doctor appointments. Oh, and my FFM, my bestie yellow-haired lady, she comes to visit and I love seeing her.

I didn't know I could love this much but I've come to love my new foster family and every time I see them I get the wiggles and wag my tail.

I've also started to talk, in my own dog language, to SFM. I think she's as excited to see me as I am to see her. I never howl or bark when left alone, I only talk in a sweet voice when she engages with me.

My favourite part is she scratches all over my face and body, even though I know it makes her sad to feel the scabs and scars. She sometimes asks me what happened to me, you know, before I came to the shelter. I don't want to tell her. I think it's obvious that I was not treated well. Maybe someone tossed me into the street because I was too sick. Maybe I was just a breeder dog in an overcrowded house. I'm not telling her because the truth would hurt her heart.

She says my teeth are not in good shape and that pugs like me should have dental treatments around the age of nine months to a year. I never got that.

Pups are Three Weeks Old

Well, my pups are getting bigger and stronger and so am I! We went to the vet and my mange is all cleared up now and I'm not in quarantine. I get to play with the other dogs if I want to. My pups, even little Mouse, are doing well. In another month or two they'll be ready for their forever home, and so will I.

I'm glad that the Paws it Forward people are going to have me spayed. I don't want any more puppies. I just want a home where I can be loved and given lots of cuddles and go for walks.

Remember that rescue organizations have lots of different dogs of all different ages and breeds. Please consider adopting from them. If you can't adopt, then fostering and donations are always welcome.

Thank you for reading my story. Who knows where life will take me from here!

Sedona,
Mama to Six

I think dogs are the most amazing creatures; they give unconditional love.

For me, they are the role model for being alive.

Gilda Radner

About the Author

Darcy Nybo began her writing journey in Grade 2 and has never looked back. She's an award-winning university-level writing instructor, a writing coach, a magazine editor, and a book editor.

She is working on her third novel and recently published a quirky book on wine grapes of the world. She also writes children's books and has three collections of short stories. You can find her books on Amazon.

As you may have guessed, Darcy loves animals, all of them. She's the kind of person who will capture an insect and put them outside. She has an unwritten agreement with spiders that they are allowed to migrate from under the house to the attic and back again at certain times of the year without harm.

In her lifetime she's been the guardian of several dogs, cats, ferrets, hamsters, cockatiels, fish and lizards. When she's not travelling, she fosters dogs because she can.

She believes that every animal deserves a chance at a good life, no matter how long that life may be.

All his life he tried to be a good person.

Many times, however, he failed.

For, after all, he was only human. He wasn't a dog.

Charles Schulz

Manufactured by Amazon.ca
Acheson, AB

14575753R10081